"The connection between the movies and business wisdom
has been there all along. It took Kevin and Michael
to bring it into sharp, digital-age focus."

Gerry Lopez, CEO, AMC Entertainment Inc.

"This wonderful book proves what I have always believed:
Movies teach us everything we need
to know in business if we would only listen."

**Beau Fraser, co-author, *Death to All Sacred Cows*
and Managing Director, The Gate Worldwide**

"*The Big Picture* updates the old adage that a (movie) picture
is worth a thousand words. A very worthwhile book."

Stu Upson, Executive Director, United States Bowling Congress

"Stew Leonard's loves stories. We are a story telling organization.
That's why *The Big Picture* will be a staple in our management's
library at Stew's. I loved it and it's a must read!"

Stew Leonard Jr., CEO, Stew Leonard's

"This is the kind of useful and enjoyable book business
people like me need to share in our companies."

Robert Phillips, President, California Tortilla Group, Inc.

"*The Big Picture* will open your mind about the power of storytelling,
whether it's for a speech, a business presentation, or a one-on-one with
a business associate or a member of your family. Great job, Kevin and
Michael. You have given me a new reason to go to the movies."

Jim Donald, CEO, Haggen, Inc. and former CEO, Starbucks Coffee Company

"To enjoy a film is a treat! To add to that by learning a valuable business
lesson from that film is a profit. To be steered to achieve both a treat
and a profit by reading *The Big Picture* is a true adventure!"

**Senator Feargal Quinn, founder of Superquinn and
former President of EuroCommerce**

"Michael and Kevin have written an informative and useful
business book that's also fun to read and easy to apply.
What a creative approach to business."

**Thom Blischok, President, Consulting & Innovation,
Information Resources, Inc.**

THE BIG PICTURE

Essential
Business Lessons
from the
Movies

Sue —
Keep Thinking Big!
Cheers!

K

From *The Godfather* to *Young Frankenstein*: Lessons in
Leadership, Marketing, and Surviving the Workplace

THE BIG
PICTURE

Essential
Business Lessons
from the
Movies

KEVIN COUPE
MICHAEL SANSOLO

BRIGANTINE MEDIA

Published by: Brigantine Media
211 North Avenue, Saint Johnsbury, Vermont 05819

Cover and Book Design by: GKS Creative

Printed in Canada

ISBN 978-0-9711542-8-5

Other Brigantine Media books include:
Am I The Leader I Need To Be? by Harold C. Lloyd
Business Success in Tough Times by Adrienne Raphel, Neil Raphel, and Janis Raye
Win the Customer, NOT the Argument by Don Gallegos
Selling Rules! by Murray Raphel
Crowning the Customer by Feargal Quinn

For more information on these books please contact:
Brigantine Media
211 North Avenue, Saint Johnsbury, Vermont 05819
Phone: 802-751-8802
Email: neil@brigantinemedia.com
Website: www.brigantinemedia.com

For Laura, who believed in all of my dreams
long past their expiration dates.
And for David, Brian, and Allison…with whom
it has been great fun growing older but not up.

Kevin Coupe

To Sarah for the poems; Corey for the symphonies;
and Janice for the confidence, companionship, and cookies.

Michael Sansolo

Contents

Take One: ACTION/ADVENTURE

003   Denial is Never a Good Idea
      Jaws

006   Play to Your Strengths
      Pirates of the Caribbean: The Curse of the Black Pearl

009   Never Get Stale…or Boring
      Casino Royale/Quantum of Solace

012   Know Your Place
      Sean Connery Movies

016   Tell Truth to Power
      Star Trek V: The Final Frontier

019   Eliminate Pre-Conceived Notions
      Star Trek VI: The Undiscovered Country

023   Take Responsibility
      The Guns of Navarone

026   Ignorance Can Get You Killed
      Butch Cassidy and the Sundance Kid

031   Find a Vision and Make it Work
      The Right Stuff

035   Go the Distance
      Rocky

Take Two: BIOPIC/DOCUMENTARY

041   Find a Role Model
      Gandhi/Schindler's List

046   Celebrate Diversity
      Selena

049   Never Underestimate Your Competition
      Tucker: The Man and His Dream

053   Shape Perception to Succeed
      Pumping Iron

Take Three: CLASSICS

059   Business Exists in the Real World
      Citizen Kane

062   Don't Take the Uneducated Risk
      Guys and Dolls/Tin Cup

065   Don't Breathe Your Own Exhaust
      All About Eve/Misery

068   Make the Best of a Bad Boss
      The Caine Mutiny/Mister Roberts

072   Do the Right Thing
      High Noon/Appaloosa

075   Stick to the Fundamentals
      Casablanca

079   Understand the Consequences of Your Actions
      The Bridge on the River Kwai/Jurassic Park

Take Four: COMEDY

085   Be Different
Babe

088   In Tough Times, Quality Wins
A League of Their Own

091   Be the Customer
Big

094   Vision Trumps All
The Producers

098   Romance Your Customers
The Wedding Singer/50 First Dates

101   Everybody Needs a Fish Story
Tootsie

104   Nearly Everyone Can Become a Leader
Renaissance Man

108   Go the Opposite Way
Young Frankenstein

111   Make the Right Decisions
Defending Your Life

114   Take a New Perspective
Working Girl

118   Anyone Can Be a Hero
Charlie Wilson's War

121   Don't Run Your Life and Business by the Numbers
Stranger Than Fiction

124   You Can Succeed Without a Gold Medal
Cool Runnings

127   Don't be Foolishly Consistent
Talladega Nights: The Legend of Ricky Bobby

Take Five: DATE MOVIES

133   Cross The Thin Line Between Good and Great
Bull Durham

137   Use Word-of-Mouth Advertising
When Harry Met Sally

140   Don't Be a One-Hit Wonder
That Thing You Do!

143   Be the Exception, Not the Rule
He's Just Not That Into You

146   Allow for the Possibility You Are Wrong
Sex and the City

149   Stiff Competition Can Eat You Up
You've Got Mail/Julie & Julia

Take Six: DRAMA

155   Protect Your Brand
American Gangster

158   Get Busy Living
The Shawshank Redemption

161   Make Sure Your Words Count
Hoosiers

165   Challenge What You Know
In the Heat of the Night

168   Art and Commerce Can Co-Exist
Big Night

172   Know the Value of Ethics and Truth
Broadcast News/Good Night, and Good Luck

176   Travel the Road Less Taken
Amadeus

179   Find the Magic
Bottle Shock

182   Take the Long View
All the President's Men/Network

186   This is Business, Not Personal
The Godfather

Establishing Shot

by Kevin Coupe

As with any endeavor worth pursuing, I believe it always is a lot more fun and fulfilling when there is passion behind it as well as logic. (That would be Jim Kirk's argument to Spock, and I embrace it.) And it is why I was thrilled to work on this book with Michael.

I love movies.

Always have. Since I was a kid, even though my parents didn't really go to movies very much and didn't understand my obsession with them. So I made movies in high school with a good friend of mine (I'll never forget Rich Davis splicing together Super-8 film trying to make action sequences work), I went to acting school (and eventually had to leave because I refused to do nude scenes), and then went to Loyola Marymount University in Los Angeles to study filmmaking and to write movie reviews for the campus newspaper.

It didn't work out, though. In part, it was because I may not have been talented enough. And, to be honest, I probably didn't *need* it enough—I wanted to do it, but was just middle class enough with sufficient Irish Catholic guilt to be unwilling to go through all the sacrifices necessary to be in the film industry.

While I opted for a career as a writer—first for a daily newspaper, then for a succession of public relations agencies and business magazines about retailing, as well as producing a video series about retailing—I also got the chance to spend some time on studio back lots and movie sets. At one point in my career, I actually worked as a bodyguard for Farrah Fawcett (I was 30 years younger and 30 pounds lighter, and luckily was never asked to anything remotely dangerous except carry her on my back once), and even wrote an episode of the French animated television series, "Barnyard Commandos" (in English, thank goodness). And I wrote dozens of movie scripts that gathered dust on shelves and in drawers, though I did have a wonderful day in Los Angeles once when Stanley Tucci and his producer took me to some studios to shop around a script I'd written, albeit without result.

In this book, however, all the strands come together. It comes both out of a love for the movies and an endless series of conversations we've had about lessons and morals to be drawn from films we'd seen. And it follows a pattern that I've established on my business website and blog, *MorningNewsBeat.com*, in which I regularly use pop culture references to explain or comment upon stories or trends that I believe are important or noteworthy. Movies and old TV series come up all the time, in the same way that I referenced two beloved *Star Trek* characters in the first paragraph of this essay. (The other constant reference point is the collected works of Jimmy Buffett, who has provided much of the soundtrack for my fantasy life).

For me, the process of co-writing this book has been a real gift—to sit down with movies both old and new and remember the pleasure of seeing them for the first time, and recapture the way they encouraged me to think differently about issues and challenges.

That's the goal here, ultimately. To use moments from a wide variety of entertainments—comedies and dramas that range from the sublime to the absurd—to illustrate how one can and should think about business matters. To look at the big picture, and to see the bigger picture in fresh perspective, both in terms of how business should operate and how business people—leaders and managers both—should innovative within them.

And now…Action!

The Power of the Movies

by Michael Sansolo

Far more than she wishes, Shelley Broader, the former president of both Michaels craft stores and Sweetbay Supermarkets, finds herself quoting Yoda, the Jedi Master of *Star Wars*.

It happens when she's counseling an employee who she sees drifting into bad habits. She sits the employee down and has a little talk about the Force. (If somehow you managed to miss all six *Star Wars* movies, the Force is the invisible power in the universe linking all objects together including space itself.)

Just as Yoda instructs his students, Broader says there are two paths to choose from: the light side, which requires discipline and commitment, but leads to happiness and peace; or the dark side, which leads to staggering problems in every *Star Wars* movie. Of course, the path to the dark side is always easiest.

With that metaphor, Broader teaches that the easy choice is the wrong one. Skills such as guiding people, building business, and serving customers all require the ability to make the tough but better choice.

To make her point, Broader echoes Yoda. And she's not alone in using a compelling story from a famous movie to motivate employees.

This book is about the business lessons found in movies. We hope that by reading our book you will look at movies in a new way. You'll appreciate that these great and compelling stories contain lessons that can make an important contribution to your business life.

Bill McEwan, the CEO of Sobey's supermarkets in Canada, once told me he thinks every CEO must be a storyteller. The ability to share the story of success and goals helps us communicate to employees and customers who we are and what makes us special. Without a narrative, executives cannot create the image of goals the company must have.

Joe Gibbs, the Hall of Fame coach of the Washington Redskins and the owner of a successful NASCAR team, preaches a similar message. Gibbs talks about how a head coach needs to tell a story that helps bind all his players to the game plan. It was his way to help a 300-pound lineman understand the importance of spending 60 minutes charging full speed into an equally large man. In NASCAR, the narrative helps the team changing the tires understand the importance of their jobs relative to the more glamorous work of the driver.

Narratives and story telling make things work in far more critical cases. When Robert McNamara died in 2009, one newspaper talked about the importance of a narrative when it comes to war. A nation must understand the story of why it is at war and what the purpose of the bloody venture might be. In short, the paper concluded, McNamara neglected his narrative for the war in Vietnam.

Most of us don't have all the stories we need or can't tell them well enough. And that's where the movies can help. Consider Broader's story about the dark side. Now Broader is an excellent storyteller, but even she couldn't paint a picture as vivid as the dark side in *Star Wars*. With that simple story, everyone she talks to will instantly think the same thing—do I really want to be Darth Vader?

A movie can inspire a CEO as well as a company's employees. A few years back, Doug Rauch, then the president of Trader Joe's supermarkets, told me about *The Wave*, a movie about surfing. *The Wave*, Rauch said, is a wonderful metaphor for business.

To succeed at surfing, the surfer must pick the right wave at the right moment. And just as importantly, you need to know when to get off the wave and move on. Making the choice on either end—getting on or getting off—is anything but easy.

This one short metaphor explained why business success is so fleeting. All it took was a movie, and in this case, a movie that was pretty obscure and that I had never seen.

Many of us use movie examples in our personal lives. We get into situations that require some direction, and we use the movies to help us out with a dramatic speech or a concise example. Meghan O'Brien, an economist from Iowa State University, described the challenge facing the Obama administration in dealing with the Great Recession. Economics may be dry, but movies aren't. She summoned up the scene from *Apollo 13*, when the crippled spaceship is returning to earth and the astronauts and the control staff in Houston discuss the difficult maneuver of bringing the ship back to earth. The key is finding just the right trajectory to avoid burning up on re-entry or bouncing off the atmosphere into space. Fixing the economy would require a similar move—and O'Brien explained it with a movie.

The inspiration for this book came from yet another real example, this one very close to home.

One day I received a phone call from my sister, Robin, who sounded very frustrated. Robin is a wonderful middle school math teacher who is also in the leadership of her district's union. In that role she has to get involved in some nasty personnel battles.

Robin told me she entered one of these meetings on an employee issue thinking she had the evidence on her side. She was sure the union would prevail. Once they got behind closed doors, the school superintendent explained a key fact the teacher in question neglected to share. In one moment, Robin's watertight arguments were blown to bits.

She said it reminded her of the scene in *The Godfather* when Michael Corleone meets the family's archenemy in a restaurant where he plans to kill him. Sonny, Michael's brother, reminds his henchman that they had better plant a gun in the restaurant's bathroom for his brother. In colorful language he tells them he wants his brother to have something other than his sexual organ in his hands when he leaves the bathroom. In other words, he'd better be properly armed.

In the middle of her meeting with the superintendent, Robin understood Sonny's concern.

Robin is possibly the smartest person I know. She's well educated, well traveled, and very well read. For 30 years, her students have benefited from her decision to dedicate her life to teaching algebra instead of making tons of money in business. More than anyone I know, she's capable of pulling an example from a wealth of background.

But the scene from *The Godfather* worked best. It was expressive, concise, and provided an image I could completely understand and appreciate.

That is what this book aims to do. We distill important business lessons from movies we like. As Kevin and I worked through this book, our hardest decision was figuring out what movies to leave out. The more we worked, the more we realized that almost any movie, even a bad one, provides excellent fodder for discussion on business values, strategy, management, and more.

We hope this book will trigger new discussions inside companies using a backdrop that everyone can easily grasp, appreciate, and even add to. Enjoy the examples we provide and keep thinking about how these movies or others you have seen relate to your business.

May the Force be with you.

"Take One"

ACTION / ADVENTURE

Denial is Never
a Good Idea

L	**LEADERSHIP**
P	**PLANNING**
Suggested for all business audiences	

JAWS IS ONE OF THE BEST THRILLERS EVER MADE, but it also serves up an example of business behavior that is almost inevitably fatal: denial.

"I don't think either one of you are aware of our problems," Mayor Vaughn (Murray Hamilton) says to Chief of Police Martin Brody (Roy Scheider) and Matt Hooper (Richard Dreyfuss) at one point in the movie. "I'm only trying to say that Amity is a summer town. We need summer dollars. Now, if the people can't swim here, they'll be glad to swim at the beaches of Cape Cod, the Hamptons, Long Island..."

Sure, Amity needed summer dollars. But what Vaughn ignored was the fact that the town also needed tourists who weren't worried about being torn limb from limb.

Vaughn's reluctance to close the beach is an example of the type of short-term thinking that should be avoided in the business world. Vaughn is working under the premise that if the town of Amity closes the beaches because of concerns about shark attacks, it will scare away the tourists on which the town depends. Which is true. But Vaughn ignores the cold reality that if tourists find out that there is a shark in the water and the town allowed people to go swimming, not only will they stay away in droves, they'll also lose trust in the town's management and never come back.

Businesses have to engender trust in their customers. Violate that sense of trust by ignoring the obvious facts—or even just the likely trends—and the repercussions can be both serious and long lasting.

Mayor Vaughn obviously never learned from the management at Johnson & Johnson, who, when faced with evidence that Tylenol had been tampered with in 1982, immediately pulled the product off the shelves. The Tylenol executives figured that they could survive the short-term hit, but would never survive the backlash if they denied the seriousness of the problem. When a new tamper-proof version of Tylenol came back to store shelves, there remained a sense of trust on the part of the consumers because Johnson & Johnson played it straight.

To be fair, although Mayor Vaughn generally is painted as the bad guy in *Jaws* because he ignores the sharp-toothed reality swimming just off shore, almost everybody is in some sort of denial. While this denial drives the plot forward, it also offers a primer on how to not deal with serious or even not-so-serious business situations.

Think about it. Quint, the great shark hunter played to crusty perfection by Robert Shaw, continues to chase the enormous great white shark with a small boat and just two crewmen. That's world-class denial.

Hooper, the oceanic expert with a passion for sharks, shows a sense of denial several times when he gets into the water with the shark. Sure, he's getting into an anti-shark cage, but the evidence is pretty strong that it isn't going to be nearly "anti" enough.

"You go inside the cage"? Quint asks. "Cage goes in the water, you go in the water. Shark's in the water. Our shark." And then he sings: "Farewell and adieu to you, fair Spanish ladies. Farewell and adieu, you ladies of Spain. For we've received orders for to sail back to Boston. And so nevermore shall we see you again."

About the only main character who doesn't seem to be in denial is Chief Brody, and even he has a moment of self-delusion when he's asked why, if he is scared of the water, he lives on an island. "It's only an island when you look at it from the water," he says.

Yeah, right.

But it also is Brody who has the movie's primal moment of clarity. It's when he's shoveling bait into the water and gets his first close-up look at the shark's massive body, black eyes, and very, very sharp teeth.

"I think we're going to need a bigger boat," he says.

Truer words never have been spoken.

In business, as in *Jaws*, denial can get you eaten for lunch.

Play to Your Strengths

B	BRANDING
RB	**RULE BREAKERS**
L	LEADERSHIP
Suggested for all business audiences	

RARELY DOES A MOVIE PRESENT ITS BUSINESS LESSONS as easily as the first *Pirates of the Caribbean.* And it does so in a package that is great fun to watch.

Pirates of the Caribbean provides two great lessons: one for marketers and one for anyone running a business. You should heed both lessons lest your business be forced to walk the plank. These lessons come from the same character, the pirate Captain Jack Sparrow, wonderfully portrayed by Johnny Depp.

The plot of the movie is actually very simple, as might be expected of a movie created around a ride at Disneyland. Sparrow is searching for the ship stolen out from under him. The ship's crew and new captain are searching for a way to break the curse that has destroyed their lives. And in a British seaport, the governor's daughter and an apprentice blacksmith are trying to find a way to make their unstated love a reality. It is all very funny and backed by a spectacular score.

Early on, we meet Captain Sparrow and can quickly tell things have taken a turn for the worse. His ship stolen in a mutiny, Sparrow now commands a dinghy, which sinks almost immediately. Through a series of quick events he comes to rescue the governor's daughter, Elizabeth Swann, from certain drowning. Instead of being thanked, however, Sparrow is set upon by British soldiers who recognize him as a pirate.

The British commander sizes up Sparrow and mocks his gun with a single bullet, his compass with no markings, his lack of a boat, and pronounces him, "The worst pirate I have ever heard of."

To which Sparrow replies, "But you have heard of me."

In short, the marketer's dream. Good or bad, you have to get your name out and known in public. Certainly, everyone wants a good name, a good reputation and a good connection with the consumer, but Sparrow's words ring true. There are countless pirates in the Caribbean and countless products and services you compete with. So ask yourself: does anyone know your name? If not, how will you change that?

Which takes us to lesson two. In the course of events, Sparrow has two sword fights with the apprentice blacksmith, Will Turner, played by Orlando Bloom. The first time they duel, Turner is clearly superior, but loses when Sparrow suddenly pulls a pistol from his belt and Turner surrenders. (A similar fight is one of the most memorable scenes in the first *Indiana Jones* movie. A guy starts swinging a big sword around Harrison Ford, who just pulls out his gun and shoots him dead.)

The second sword fight takes place on a ship and Sparrow unleashes a boom that knocks Turner overboard. Frustrated, Turner taunts Sparrow that "you'd never beat me in a fair fight." Sparrow's reply says it all: "That's hardly incentive to fight fair."

Exactly! Who says we have to fight fair? Just like Captain Sparrow, we want to fight in a way that improves our chances to win. Of course, unlike Sparrow, we can't cheat to make that happen.

Too many businesses make the mistake of fighting on the wrong ground by attacking their competitor's strength. There are, for example, numerous retailers who ran themselves out of business by attacking Walmart on price. In short, they brought a sword to a duel where the other guy had a gun. They can't win in a fight against a company with advantages of logistics and economies of scale.

Over time, and from painful experience, some smart retailers learned that the way to co-exist with or even beat Walmart was to do things the giant retailer could not. Competitors played up the virtue of their smaller-sized stores, or their specialty services, or their unique products. Trader Joe's, Costco, and even Whole Foods are great examples of retailers who found a separate niche from Walmart and attracted customers by doing what Walmart doesn't.

Competitive scenarios in business rarely play out as simply as a movie conflict. Instead, it requires hard work to figure out your opponents' strengths and weaknesses. It requires constant effort to reinforce your own strengths and to minimize or correct your own weaknesses.

Sparrow offers us words of advice. As he tells Will Turner, the world revolves on our ability to understand what we can and cannot do. Once we face our own strengths and limitations honestly, we can sail on into the future.

Yo-ho.

Never Get Stale
...or Boring

B	BRANDING
RB	RULE BREAKERS

Suggested for all business audiences

THE NEARLY TOTAL REINVENTION OF THE JAMES BOND MOVIES, beginning with *Casino Royale* in 2006 and following through with *Quantum of Solace* in 2008, is just the kind of artistic shift needed to shake and stir moviegoers. It's also a great example of what businesses sometimes need to do—take risks, even multimillion-dollar risks, to avoid getting stale and even irrelevant.

Let's face it. By the time Pierce Brosnan ended his tenure as 007, the series had completely lost touch with reality. Not that it ever was designed to be a realistic depiction of the world of espionage, but in the first three movies—*Dr. No, From Russia With Love*, and *Goldfinger*—there was some effort to present a world that was at least vaguely recognizable. (Especially *From Russia With Love*, which remains my favorite of the first twenty Bond films.) But after that, the movies got crazier and more outlandish. Now, to be fair, the producers were responding to what people wanted—more special effects, more gadgets, more over-the-top villains. So the Bond producers did what you're supposed to do in business: act on the presumption that the customer is always right.

The problem was that at a certain point, they couldn't top themselves anymore. The invisible car in *Die Another Day* was the straw that broke the camel's back for a lot of us. Where could they go from there?

At the same time, while James Bond was driving around in invisible cars, Matt Damon as Jason Bourne and Kiefer Sutherland as Jack Bauer were creating grittier yet equally entertaining spies in the movies and on television. Next to them, James Bond didn't seem so tough. He just seemed sort of...irrelevant. And soft. And not all that interesting.

Now, the producers clearly were not sure how to restart the franchise, and *Die Another Day* shows the franchise in flux. In the first half-hour, the movie portrays James Bond being captured by North Korean soldiers and tortured for months before being repatriated in a prisoner exchange by spy chief M. Good stuff, until they lost their bearings and introduced a character played by Madonna, and allowed the movie to devolve into just another flick about a megalomaniac who wants to take over the world. (Though it does have Halle Berry in a bikini, which is actually the movie's best special effect—far more impressive than that damned invisible car.)

That was in 2002, and the producers waited until 2006 to introduce a new Bond—Daniel Craig—and a new approach to the character and the films. This Bond was the "blunt instrument" described by Ian Fleming in the original books. He was shorter and blonder than any of the Bonds who preceded him, which made some fans crazy, but he also was significantly tougher and actually looked like someone who might be dangerous with a license to kill.

Craig didn't have Sean Connery's deadly irony, George Lazenby's kilt, Roger Moore's safari suits, Timothy Dalton's Shakespearean intensity, or Pierce Brosnan's uncommon good looks. There was no "Q," no Miss Moneypenny, no ironic quips.

All the better. *Casino Royale* wasn't just the best James Bond movie in decades, it also was a really good thriller—taut and action-packed, with characters who are more human than iconic. The movie rebooted the Bond franchise, going back to the character's roots and exploring what made him what he is. There were knowing winks about the character's future, but it left open the possibility that the producers will continue to take the series in this direction.

Which they did with *Quantum of Solace*. Daniel Craig's second go-round as James Bond wasn't nearly as well reviewed as *Casino Royale*. It was the shortest (106 minutes) Bond movie ever made, the only direct sequel to a previous Bond movie, and was considerably more violent. Now, I happened to like it—a lot. Mostly because the producers seemed to be experimenting with the ideas a bit, seeing what worked and what didn't. And while the critics didn't always approve, moviegoers did, and the movie made more than a half-billion dollars in box office receipts globally.

Big risk, big reward.

Staying stagnant isn't an option—whether you are running a retail store, operating a service business, or producing James Bond movies.

In fact, this is a pretty good metaphor if you are running a business. If your operation begins to feel like Roger Moore—good natured but slow, flabby, and wearing a leisure suit—it's time to begin thinking like Daniel Craig. Which is to say, lean, muscular, and both efficient and effective—the perfect kind of business model for a challenging business environment.

SEAN CONNERY MOVIES:
THE WIND AND THE LION (1975)
THE MAN WHO WOULD BE KING (1975)
ROBIN AND MARIAN (1976)
THE UNTOUCHABLES (1987)

Know Your Place

B	BRANDING
RB	**RULE BREAKERS**
P	**PLANNING**
Suggested for all business audiences	

FORGET ABOUT HIS JAMES BOND.

In the mid-1970s Sean Connery made three movies that represent a distinctive and iconic view of masculinity and heroism. But in each case, Connery's character is undermined by time or by errors in judgment linked to a specific and flawed view of the world. In my view, that makes these movies more compelling than Connery's classic portrayal of 007. These movies are wonderful object lessons for the modern businessperson, who may be tempted even in the 21st century to make testosterone-fueled decisions.

The first of these films was *The Wind and The Lion*, in which Connery played Mulai Ahmed er Raisuli, also known as the "Last of the Barbary Pirates." The movie takes place in Morocco at the beginning of the 20th century, as the French, British, and German governments are all seeking a political beachhead in northern Africa. Outraged over what he views as the Sultan's obeisance to the Europeans, Raisuli decides to kidnap an American woman, Eden Pedecaris (Candice Bergen), and her son, hoping to provoke a political incident and embarrass the Sultan. He doesn't count on the growing might of the United States and President Theodore Roosevelt's willingness to flex his muscles.

The movie has some wonderful performances (especially Brian Keith as Roosevelt). The business lesson comes at the very end of the film, when Raisuli writes a letter to Roosevelt after the situation has been resolved and the two men have come to respect each other even over thousands of miles. The letter reads:

"You are like the wind and I like the lion. You form the tempest. The sand stings my eyes and the ground is parched. I roar in defiance but you do not hear. But between us there is a difference. I, like the lion, must remain in my place. While you, like the wind, will never know yours."

In terms of business, I am reminded of how small hardware stores try to compete with a company like Lowe's, which is like the "wind" that does not seem to know its place. To compete with any large and dominant competitor, it is critical to understand the rules of the game. You cannot compete by trying to do what the big guy does. You have to do something different, something that distinguishes you from the larger competitor. To think that you can do the same thing, and generate the same results, is to ignore the reality of the situation.

The second Connery movie, also released in 1975, is *The Man Who Would Be King*, director John Huston's adaptation of the Rudyard Kipling story. In this movie, set in the late 1800's, Connery plays Daniel Dravot, who, along with Peachey Carnehan (Michael Caine), decides to travel from British-controlled India to Kafiristan, which borders Pakistan and Afghanistan, a site no white man had visited since Alexander the Great. There, they believe, their superior intellect will allow them to set themselves up as kings and dominate the land.

Their plan works up to a point, and that's where the business lesson comes in. When the Kafir people decide that Dravot and Carnehan are gods, not just kings, Connery's Dravot begins to almost believe it and starts acting in a way that ultimately will put both their plan and their lives in danger. That's a critical mistake that a lot of businesses make: they take their eye off the ball, and develop delusions of grandeur that reality cannot support. It is the point where ambition becomes hubris, and it is the point that every businessperson must avoid.

Carnehan puts it in succinct, if earthy, terms: "Danny's only a man. But he breaks wind at both ends simultaneous—which is more, I reckon, than any god can do."

And more than any businessperson should.

The third of the mid-seventies movies is actually my sentimental favorite, though the business lesson to be gleaned from it is a little less specific. *Robin and Marian* is a charming, romantic movie about Robin Hood (Connery) and Maid Marian (Audrey Hepburn) in late middle age, after Robin has returned from the Crusades, dissatisfied with the notion that his best days are behind him. This aging and balding Robin Hood keeps looking for the next big adventure, the next battle, the next act of heroism that can define his life and manhood. It's a lovely movie, with resonant performances, especially by Nicol Williamson as Little John, and Robert Shaw as the Sheriff of Nottingham, who is far more accepting than Robin Hood that time may have passed both him and his old enemy by.

Know your limits. That's a pretty good business lesson, after all.

Another Connery movie with an important business lesson came a decade later and actually netted him a Best Supporting Actor Oscar. In *The Untouchables*, Connery plays Jimmy Malone, an incorruptible Chicago cop.

Asked by federal agent Elliot Ness to join his task force seeking to get the goods on Al Capone, Malone utters some of the best lines in the movie, and ones that ought to serve as the marching orders for every business competing with another:

"What are you prepared to do? If you open the can on these worms you must be prepared to go all the way. Because they're not gonna give up the fight, until one of you is dead…You wanna know how to get Capone? They pull a knife, you pull a gun. He sends one of yours to the hospital, you send one of his to the morgue. That's the Chicago way! And that's how you get Capone."

The business message is simple. "Compete" is a verb, and competition is a deadly serious business that requires a willingness to do everything and anything to come out on top.

As Malone says elsewhere in the movie: "Here endeth the lesson."

Tell Truth to Power

RB	RULE BREAKERS
E	ETHICS
Suggested for all business audiences	

FROM EARLY CHILDHOOD OUR PARENTS give us contradictory advice. They urge us to tell the truth. We're told the story of how George Washington admitted to cutting down his father's cherry tree and we are motivated to practice honesty. (It's a myth, but heck, we're kids.) We read *The Emperor's New Clothes* and see the power of a simple truth uttered by a child.

Then, almost as quickly, those same parents teach us about the "white lie," a falsehood uttered to spare the feelings of a relative in a horrible outfit, a neighbor with a bad haircut—seemingly harmless fibs designed to spare the feelings of others. In short, we're told there are times we shouldn't tell the truth. Then we grow up and need therapy.

In business, the notion of truth telling gets even tougher, especially when the person we need to confront is the boss. The concept is called "telling truth to power;" being willing to risk your job, career, reputation, and more for the simple audacious act of telling the truth. And often, many of us fail this key test and choose the easy path into a white lie. Telling truth to power is frequently a short-time mission if the boss doesn't appreciate your candor.

Despite the danger to your continued employment or popularity, telling the truth can make all the difference in a company's success. It can alert higher-ups to a problem or mistake that might doom the future of the company. It might well be the way to alert the Emperor that his new clothes aren't really there.

Luckily for us, the movies provide the perfect example. *Star Trek* isn't a series that attracts casual fans. There are the devoted Trekkers who worship the television shows and movies in great detail, finding wisdom throughout. And even among the general population, *Star Trek* is one of the most popular cultural phenomena of all time.

The lessons *Star Trek* provides for business are numerous. For example, in the 1960s it seemed beyond imagination that Captain James T. Kirk could whip a small communication device out of his pocket, flip it open and call his ship. Today we call that device a cell phone.

Star Trek V: The Final Frontier features one scene that should be must-see viewing for every underling who ever wondered about the need to tell truth to power. It provides a stunning reminder that sometimes a hard question needs to be asked. And once asked, the truth becomes clear to everyone. (One piece of truth here about me: I am enough of a Trekker to know that all even numbered *Star Trek* movies are better than those with odd numbers. But this lesson comes from one of the lesser movies.)

The story finds the heroes of the Starship Enterprise hijacked and taken to a part of space thought unreachable. To add intrigue to the plot, the hijacker is Sybok, the half-brother of Spock, the Enterprise's logic-driven, Vulcan first officer. His method of hijacking is unusual: looking into the mind of his victim and helping that person face his greatest source of grief. *Star Trek* always boldly goes where no one has gone before.

The Final Frontier is not physical, though. Sybok believes he has found God and Heaven, and using the Enterprise, he endeavors to make the journey.

Against all odds, they succeed (of course they do…it's a *Star Trek* movie) and Kirk, Spock, McCoy, and Sybok land on a desolate planet where rocks move, the ground shakes, and a image appears of a bearded and wizened face: God. And God has a request—to use the Starship Enterprise to visit the rest of the galaxy.

Which is when Kirk has the audacity to ask a simple question: "What does God need with a starship?"

The rest of his team is stunned at his impertinence, and "God" is clearly annoyed. When Kirk asks a second time, "God" shoots a bolt of energy into Kirk, knocking him to the ground. Suddenly, Kirk's challenge seems a dangerous test of authority.

Spock then takes up Kirk's question and is also shot with a bolt. When challenged again, "God" reveals that he isn't some divine being in Heaven, but a prisoner long held on this planet. And he needs a starship to escape.

It's hardly spoiling the plot to reveal that he doesn't deprive the crew of their spaceship. After all, they couldn't have made all the additional *Star Trek* movies if the key characters were killed on a distant world.

But the lesson matters. Bringing truth to a more powerful colleague or superior is never without risks. The bigger risk is in asking nothing. How many companies have slid into disastrous decisions because no one challenged top management or pointed out some contradictory information that might have held the key to a better decision? Think Enron, Lehman Brothers, AIG. How many mistakes have been made when silence is considered to be golden and questions are an annoyance?

How many bosses have wrongly greeted employee's questions with all the warmth of the false "God" in *Star Trek V*? Instead of answering or welcoming the question, the questioner is knocked down with a bolt—a sharp rebuke, discipline, or worse.

In short, we should want someone to tell us that our new product may have flaws, that our marketing strategy may have a problem, that our "new clothes" don't exist.

We need Captain Kirk to ask the tough question.

Eliminate Pre-Conceived Notions

E	ETHICS
L	LEADERSHIP
P	PLANNING
Suggested for all business audiences	

FIRST OF ALL, I have to say that I am distressed that Michael decided to include *Star Trek V: The Final Frontier* in his list of movies. While I am a fan of most things *Star Trek*, it seems obvious to me that the fifth film in the series is a pretty awful movie, and it is hard for me to imagine that it could be a business lesson for anything.

But there are some excellent lessons in *Star Trek VI,* which is one of the best movies in the series, in part because that movie is connected to something outside the original television series and its mythology. *Star Trek VI* has subtle references to Shakespeare, the fall of the Soviet Union, and even Richard Nixon.

The main theme of *Star Trek VI* is the importance of eliminating pre-conceived notions. The crew of the Starship Enterprise is assigned to escort a group of Klingons into space controlled by the United Federation of Planets. The Klingons have suffered an enormous environmental disaster that threatens to destroy their culture, and they need diplomatic relations with the Federation in order to survive. The whole thing is a metaphor for the fall of Communism and the Berlin

Wall and it works exceptionally well.

While there are great space battles, the movie's real message is about prejudice. Captain James T. Kirk, who commands the Enterprise, hates the Klingons, fueled by the fact that they killed his son. He has been fighting them for decades. He cannot get past that bias. He cannot imagine a universe in which Klingons are allies and not villains. His bias threatens to undermine the ship's mission, and puts him in conflict with his friend and first officer, Spock, who sees the logic of bringing the Klingons into the Federation. Spock, of course, has his own blind spots because he is so devoted to logic that he cannot conceive of the conspiracy that actually threatens peace between the Federation and the Klingons. At one point, Spock looks at Kirk and says, "Is it possible, you and I, that we have grown so inflexible as to have outlived our usefulness?"

Inflexibility, which is what happens when you prejudge a situation, is a terrible characteristic to bring to business. It limits your options and makes it difficult to reach the kind of judgments necessary to thrive in any kind of situation.

A real-life example in which inflexibility led to a company missing a business opportunity is the decision by Tesco, the biggest and most successful retailer in the U.K. as well as the third-ranked retailer in the world, to enter the U.S. market. There had been rumors for years that Tesco wanted to come to the U.S., and then the retailer did a year of market research in California before opening up a chain of small grocery stores called Fresh & Easy.

It wasn't like Klingons invading Earth, but it was close.

The Fresh & Easy stores opened by Tesco in Southern California, Arizona, and Nevada were small—between 10,000 and 15,000 square feet—and by American standards, had a high percentage of private label items (products that carried the Fresh & Easy name, not that of Kraft or some other consumer packaged goods manufacturer). This was mistake number one, since Americans have never been as open to private label as in Europe, where they do a much higher percentage of sales. This is changing, as the recession has made people more accepting of private label, which tends to be less expensive. But for Fresh & Easy's purposes, the recession may have come a year too late.

Fresh & Easy also liked to sell its fresh fruits and vegetables already packaged, as opposed to loose in bins, which is how Americans like them. Again, this was a system that came over from Tesco's U.K. stores, where customers were used to it and it was seen as both efficient and effective. Not so in the U.S., I'm afraid. The company also sold a number of products and flavors unfamiliar to U.S. shoppers, in part because it brought some of its U.K. suppliers over to the U.S. and set them up in business. This inattention to American preferences reinforces the bubble within which the company seemed to be operating.

And while Tesco in the U.K. has had a long history of accumulating customer data and employing shopper-specific marketing techniques, for reasons that have never been entirely clear, it did not use these systems in the U.S., perhaps because it wrongly believed that its market research was good enough.

The result was that Fresh & Easy had a somewhat alien countenance, and never was able to get the kind of traction that Tesco needed in order to open enough stores to achieve critical mass. Its inflexibility—its prejudging of the situation and working from biases that undermined its mission—put Tesco in the position where it finally had to admit that it had made some serious mistakes in the U.S. (The recession didn't help, since Tesco hadn't put enough of an emphasis on low prices, and low prices were precisely what recession-era customers demanded.)

At the end of *Star Trek VI: The Undiscovered Country*, Kirk and Spock realize that they have been made inflexible by their own biases, and they transcend them and take actions that, well, save the galaxy.

Likewise, at this writing, Tesco has indicated that it is going to make changes at Fresh & Easy that it hopes can rescue its American venture. We'll see. The capacity for growth and flexibility is critical to success, whether you are a starship captain or a grocer, and you want to live long and prosper.

MICHAEL'S POINT OF VIEW (POV):

(Occasionally, Kevin and I will offer contrasting or additional perspectives on the movies the other has written about.)

A number of years ago, I heard retired Gen. Colin Powell speak about the end of the Soviet Union. He recalled being in a meeting with then-Soviet Premier Mikhail Gorbachev when he realized the latter was proposing an end to the Cold War. Powell said he wasn't entirely pleased. After all, he had grown comfortable with the Cold War and his Soviet foes. Think about geo-politics today and it's clear that the world was actually simpler when the foe was the Soviets and not fanatically motivated groups such as Al Qaeda. It's a great metaphor that sometimes we actually get comfortable with our competition or enemies, be they Klingons or Soviets.

America's Big Three automakers had a comfort level for many years battling among themselves and couldn't conceive of small Japanese cars stealing their market. ABC, NBC, and CBS competed but couldn't imagine cable networks shattering their hold on home viewership. Similar stories run throughout competition and the economy. In short, embracing the known challenges, even when they are difficult, is short sighted. Always consider the "what ifs," because often that's what happens.

Take Responsibility

L	LEADERSHIP
P	PLANNING
Suggested for all business audiences	

THE GUNS OF NAVARONE, IS A TERRIFIC EXAMPLE of how to build a team, which, as we all know, is a critical part of any business plan.

Based on the novel by Alistair McLean, *The Guns of Navarone* is the story of an Allied commando team that surreptitiously invades the island of Navarone in the Aegean Sea, charged with blowing up the enormous guns that threaten to destroy the Royal Navy ships that need to sail past it in order to rescue 2,000 forces.

Major Roy Franklin (Anthony Quayle) puts together a team of disparate personalities to accomplish the mission, led by Major Keith Mallory (Gregory Peck), who happens to be a mountain climbing expert; Corporal Miller (David Niven), an explosives expert; and Colonel Andrea Stavros (Anthony Quinn), who used to serve in the now-defeated Greek Army. (Think *Mission: Impossible* set in World War II, without the self-destructing tape.)

But once the team arrives on Navarone, things get complicated. Franklin breaks a leg and cannot go on with the mission, which leaves Mallory in charge. Miller, who happens to be a friend of Franklin, resents the whole exercise since he's a committed civilian. And Stavros has pledged to kill Mallory since earlier in the war Mallory had accidentally

23

been responsible for the deaths of his wife and children.

In other words, Mallory has his hands full. The good news is, he's played by Gregory Peck—and therefore is alternately stern, compassionate, vigorous and resourceful. He's not a killer, but he's willing to kill and be killed for the right cause. He has a wry sense of humor. Of course, while the audience never has any doubt that he's leading the team in the right direction, Miller, Stavros, and the rest of the team don't exactly share that confidence. And so, *The Guns of Navarone* really is about leadership, and how Mallory gains the confidence of his men.

The first step is to accept that he has the ultimate responsibility, even when guys like Miller go out of their way to make his life miserable. It actually is in the relationship with Miller that Mallory's leadership skills are most severely tested and ultimately proven.

At one point, Miller wonders what to do with a spy who has been discovered in their midst, and he suggests that perhaps Mallory will have to kill her, challenging his authority: "I'm not anxious to kill her, I'm not anxious to kill anyone. You see, I'm not a born soldier. I was trapped. You may find me facetious from time to time, but if I didn't make some rather bad jokes I'd go out of my mind. No, I prefer to leave the killing to someone like you, an officer and a gentleman, a leader of men."

Mallory responds by trying to find common ground: "If you think I wanted this, any of this, you're out of your mind. I was trapped like you, just like anyone who put on the uniform!"

That doesn't work. Miller keeps pressing, just like that annoying guy in the office who never likes to let go: "Of course you wanted it, you're an officer, aren't you? I never let them make me an officer! I don't want the responsibility."

And that's when Mallory draws the line, while accepting his role: "So you've had a free ride, all this time! Someone's got to take responsibility if the job's going to get done!" He explains in no uncertain terms to Miller that he also has responsibilities to the team, and he'd better live up to them: "You think you've been getting away with it all this time, standing by. Well, son, your bystanding days are over! You're in it now, up to your neck! They told me that you're a genius with explosives. Start proving it!" He shows Miller his gun and adds, "You got me in the mood to use this thing, and by God, if you don't think of something, I'll use it on you!"

From that point on, Miller pretty much falls in line. He was allowed to make his point, but when he crossed the line, Mallory exerted his authority. Threatening to kill him might be a little farther than most businesspeople would like to go, but you have to keep the exchange in context.

The biggest thing Mallory has going for him is his sense of certainty, even in rough situations. I've always thought that this is one of the most important characteristics for any leader—the ability to listen, to engage, but ultimately demonstrate commitment to and belief in whatever decision has been made. In the end, that's what wins Stavros over and persuades him not to kill Mallory. He's seen how he approaches his job, and that alleviates the driving need for revenge.

It's a pretty good business leadership lesson. It's important that the leader act like a leader if he or she wants the rest of the team to fall in step. That doesn't mean forcing blind loyalty, but rather, demonstrating your acceptance of the leadership role, and requiring others to do what's expected of them, too.

Ignorance Can Get You Killed

RB	**RULE BREAKERS**
L	**LEADERSHIP**
P	**PLANNING**
Suggested for all business audiences	

ACCORDING TO AN OLD ADAGE, the biggest problem isn't what you don't know. It's what you know that isn't so. In business, misinformation can leave you vulnerable against the competition or even unaware of what your own team is and is not capable of doing.

In the movies, it can bring laughter…and tears.

The lack of good information plays a huge role in the wonderfully offbeat western *Butch Cassidy and the Sundance Kid*, starring the incomparable duo of Paul Newman and Robert Redford.

Butch and Sundance are outlaws, robbing trains and banks with the Hole in the Wall gang. Butch is the brains of the group and Sundance the quickest and most accurate shooter around. And they delight the audience with witty dialogue and countless amusing bits of wisdom.

In one early scene, Butch is faced with a railroad safe that features an abundance of security devices aimed at thwarting him personally. Butch places a copious amount of dynamite on the safe and then watches the safe, the money, and the rail car blast into the sky. As the money slowly flutters to earth, Sundance quietly asks, "Use enough dynamite there, Butch?" It's a line every company should think of whenever plans are taken to an extreme that serve virtually no one except the ego of the person doing the job.

There are countless other laugh-out-loud moments in this movie filled with unexpected plot twists, but the lesson of information is repeated again and again.

Sundance is challenged as a cheater for winning at poker. His accuser is adamant about Sundance leaving his money on the table until he learns that his opponent is the Sundance Kid. At that point, his only question is whether the Kid is as good as everyone says. Sundance obliges by shooting a poker chip multiple times across the floor. In short, the accuser had no idea who he was up against and luckily escapes with his life.

In another scene, Butch learns Sundance can't swim at a moment when swimming is the only way to escape a difficult situation. Butch assuages Sundance's concerns by telling him, "The fall [from the cliff] will kill you." At another equally inopportune moment, Butch has to tell Sundance that he's never actually shot anyone. Sundance replies calmly, but angrily, "One hell of a time to tell me."

But the moments aren't all funny. Three in particular stand out. First, when the pair moves to Bolivia to get away from the law, it quickly becomes evident they know nothing about the country, especially the importance of speaking Spanish in South America. A second key moment comes in the movie's final scene in Bolivia. The pair is cornered in a courtyard yet believe they will get away because they can shoot their way out. Little do they know how outgunned they are.

Most pivotal is the event that sends them to South America. In the process of robbing a train the gang sees another train pull to an abrupt stop nearby. Suddenly the doors open and a posse bolts out on horseback in full gallop. As Butch, Sundance, and the gang flee, something becomes very obvious: this is not the average posse.

In the course of the chase, the posse tracks the pair over rock, through water, and past deceptions of all kinds. Repeatedly, Butch and Sundance are left asking the key question of the movie: "Who are those guys?"

It's a question that anyone in business should never ask, but all too often many do. Like Butch and Sundance, many businesses focus on the job at hand with tunnel vision. We follow *our business* and *our staff* without looking beyond to see who else might be gaining on us. In a way, it's a perverse dedication to the words of baseball pitcher Satchel Paige who once warned against looking back as something might be gaining on you.

In business, you should always be looking back, forward and to both sides.

No business can afford to get to critical situations and suddenly learn that a key employee doesn't have the skill you assumed he or she had. No business can afford to suddenly realize the complete lack of an integral skill such as the need to speak Spanish to keep business flowing.

And yet, many times we are caught short. Any retailer that doesn't have a big box store as a competitor should wake up every day thinking a giant retailer is about to announce plans to open a store nearby. Only by preparing for a competitive war at all times can you be ready for the day when that war might be real.

It may sound like paranoia and maybe it is, but at times paranoia is a valuable trait. It can keep a business sharp and fully aware of the real situation, not a fantasy. As Sundance asks Butch in one scene, "Don't you ever get tired of being wrong?" In the movie, the line is funny and helps advance the plot. In business, a similar track record is likely fatal.

No business can ever afford to survey the competition and ask, "Who are those guys?" If you do, it's likely to be a very unhappy ending.

KEVIN'S POV:
Dave Dillon, the CEO of the Kroger Co., one of the nation's top supermarket chains, recently told me that *Butch Cassidy and the*

Sundance Kid is the film he often refers to as a business metaphor.

The scene he likes to use comes near the beginning of the film, when Butch and Sundance are riding to meet the Hole in the Wall Gang, only to discover that one of the gang, Harvey Logan, is engaged in a mutiny—he wants to be in charge.

The exchange goes like this and involves Butch, Harvey, and News Carver, one of the outlaws:

BUTCH: What's the matter with you guys? When I came here, you were nothin'. You weren't even a gang. I formed ya.

HARVEY: Who says?

BUTCH: Well, read 'em a clippin', News.

NEWS: This one here's from the *Salt Lake Herald*. "Butch Cassidy's Hole in the Wall Gang..." (News keeps reading)

BUTCH: (interrupting) "Butch Cassidy's Hole in the Wall Gang"— that's me! You want Harvey to do your plannin' for ya? You want him to do your thinkin' for ya? You want him to run things? You can shut up now, News.

NEWS: Oh not yet 'til I get to the good part, Butch. "...also known to have participated in the holdup are Flat Nose Curry and News Carver." I just love readin' my name in the paper, Butch.

As Dillon says, this exchange illustrates something important—you should never believe your own press clippings. The difference between Butch, who is a natural leader, and News, who is anything but, is that Butch keeps them in context—he uses them when they serve his purpose, but knows that in order to maintain his leadership, he'll have to find a way to beat his much bigger and meaner opponent. Which he does, partly through distraction and partly by ignoring the rules when they don't serve his purpose.

There's also another important lesson here. Harvey's goal once he took over was to rob a train on both ends of its trip, figuring that once the first robbery takes place, they'll never be expecting a second robbery, which will be the more profitable one. Butch's first reaction is that this isn't a good idea, until he wins back control of the gang, and then he reconsiders, illustrating that good ideas can come from anyone, including your corporate rivals. Remember that old tenet: "anything is possible if you don't care who gets the credit."

Of course, it turns out that the second robbery isn't such a good idea after all, because it sets events in motion that put Butch and Sundance on the run. And that's another business lesson: sometimes in life there are events you can't control. At which point you have to improvise, even if improvisation means a strategic retreat.

Find a Vision and Make it Work

RB	RULE BREAKERS
L	LEADERSHIP
Suggested for all business audiences	

NOT ONLY IS *THE RIGHT STUFF* ONE OF THE BEST American movies ever made, in my opinion, but it also manages to be a microcosm of the business experience in a lot of ways—describing not just the life cycle of businesses, but also defining some of the pitfalls that businesses should do their best to avoid.

The movie, directed by Phillip Kaufman, is based on the Tom Wolfe best seller about the Mercury space program. It focuses largely on the tension that existed between the seven original astronauts and NASA, then a nascent government program that had been made a high priority by President Eisenhower, who desperately wanted to beat the Russians into space. The Mercury program was the beginning of that effort, to be followed by the Gemini and, finally, the Apollo program that resulted in U.S. astronauts landing on the moon in 1969.

The Right Stuff establishes from the outset that the guy with the real "right stuff" is test pilot Chuck Yeager (Sam Shepard), who, ironically, is not part of the astronaut corps. Among other things, he's too much of a maverick, and they are looking for corporate types who can sell the program as well as fly. The same thing often happens in business—the founder often is the visionary who has the game-changing business idea, but he may not be perceived by business types as the best person to bring the idea to market.

Once the seven astronauts are chosen for the Mercury program, management at NASA attempts to slot them into predetermined positions, which is exactly what business managers try to do with their people. Personality and idiosyncrasies are not often valued in business, and yet, as *The Right Stuff* makes clear, it is these very qualities that can give a program the best kind of differential advantage. After all, the Russian program likely was steeped in bureaucracy and highly intolerant of personality, and they still haven't been to the moon.

Deke Slayton (Scott Paulin) explains the value of the astronauts in stark terms:

"…We all heard the rumors that they want to send a monkey up first…What they're trying to do to us is send a man up to do a monkey's work. Us, a bunch of college-trained chimpanzees…we've got to change things around here…we are pilots. And we know more about what we need to fly this thing than anybody else. So what we have to do is to alter the experiment. And what that comes down to is who is gonna control this thing from here on out."

This is a valuable lesson for business leaders—they need to understand that it is critical to trust the people they have hired to get the job done, and then give them the tools and freedom to live up to their responsibilities.

Money drives everything. As Gordon Cooper (Dennis Quaid) says to Gus Grissom (Fred Ward) at one point, "Y'know what makes this bird go up? Funding makes this bird go up!" And Grissom replies, "No bucks, no Buck Rogers." To a great extent, the astronauts' greatest job is to present an image that will keep the money train rolling. They didn't call it venture capital then, but that's exactly what it was. This isn't one of the more romantic parts of running a business, but let's face it—without money, things don't go very far.

Another important lesson from the movie: if you have to choose between your job and your wife, choose the latter. The government wants to exploit John Glenn's wife for publicity purposes when he's about to take off, but Annie Glenn, afflicted with a speech impediment, wants none of it. On the phone John Glenn (Ed Harris) tells her, "Annie, listen to me, OK? You listening? If you don't want the Vice President or the TV networks or anybody else to come into the house, then that's it, as far as I'm concerned. They are not coming in, and I will back you all the way, a hundred percent on this. And you tell them that, OK? I don't want Johnson or any of the rest of them to set as much as one toe inside our house."

Good lesson.

The Right Stuff also makes the case that a really successful enterprise depends on varied talents and personalities. A cookie-cutter approach doesn't generate the kind of light and air you need to be successful. There's a moment when John Glenn is lecturing his six fellow astronauts about their sometimes irresponsible personal behavior. It is Alan Shepard (Scott Glenn) who sets him straight:

"Mr. Glenn, you are way out of line. I'd advise you not to try and foist your view of morality on anybody else in this group. Each man here has volunteered to do a job. Each man here is devoting long hours of training to prepare for it, and doing many things above and beyond the strict call of duty, such as morale tours of factories...and foregoing any semblance of an orderly family life. And Mr. Glenn, as long as a man uses good sense, what he does with his zipper or his wick is his own business!"

That may be politically incorrect, but you get the point.

Of course, as the movie goes on, despite the best efforts of the Mercury astronauts, NASA does become a little more corporate, a little more political, a little more politically correct. The government does its best to control the behavior and image of the Mercury Seven, and *The Right Stuff* makes the argument that the space program has never been the same since.

It is in losing touch with the astronauts' personal qualities, the movie argues, that the nation's space program began also to lose touch with the imaginations of Americans. And when that connection was severed, space began to seem less like a final frontier waiting to be conquered, and more like an expensive indulgence.

In all of our businesses, we should seek "the right stuff." It embodies the three qualities to make a business successful: a vision, the infrastructure, and the people to make it work.

Go the Distance

RB	RULE BREAKERS
E	ETHICS
L	LEADERSHIP
Suggested for all business audiences		

THERE ARE A LOT OF TERRIFIC MOMENTS in *Rocky*, but one of the most charming is when Adrian, the mousy pet shop employee who finds herself in an unlikely relationship with a broken-down fighter and part-time (and not very effective) leg breaker, asks Rocky Balboa, "Why do you wanna fight?"

His answer is simply: "Because I can't sing and dance."

Rocky is full of business metaphors, because it is a movie largely about desire and how far it can take you. Not necessarily to the top of the heap, of course. It isn't giving much away three decades after the movie came out to note here that Rocky doesn't win his boxing match against Apollo Creed. Rocky wants to go the distance and not embarrass himself.

In business, being number one isn't always possible—though there are plenty of companies, GE for example, that have made being number one or two in every market it serves a matter of corporate culture. That's fine...if you are GE, or any other behemoth of a company that can afford the time, money and effort to be on top of the heap.

Of course, there also are plenty of companies out there that have succeeded without being number one or two. They are plenty successful simply by being the best they can be, by offering their customers a differentiated product or service, and by going the distance. Their desire is not for supremacy, but rather for prosperity based on excellence.

An example of this kind of company is Burgerville, a wonderful fast food chain in Oregon and Washington. Burgerville is never going to be the nation's top fast food chain; it doesn't even have enough locations (39 as of this writing) to be number one in the markets it serves. But by offering a differentiated menu—"local, vegetarian-fed and antibiotic-free beef in our burgers, cage-free eggs in our breakfast items and our salads feature mixed greens with sustainable, local ingredients such as smoked salmon and Oregon hazelnuts," according to the company—Burgerville is a little company that makes a big difference. About once a year, I find myself driving from Seattle to Portland, and I make a special effort to stop at Burgerville. While I'm not a big fast food fan, I always look forward to the burgers made with real Tilamook cheese and the smoothies made with real local berries.

The food is made fresh, and you can practically taste the desire to create a better-for-you fast food experience.

I keep hoping that Burgerville will expand to the east coast, where I live, but alas, no such expansion seems to be in the cards. Like Rocky Balboa, Burgerville knows what neighborhood it is from, and is focused on achieving excellence in that marketplace.

There is another business lesson that can be found in *Rocky*—this one in the story behind the movie.

It is a well-known Hollywood tale that when Sylvester Stallone wrote the original script for *Rocky*, numerous studios wanted to buy it as a vehicle for various star actors such as Burt Reynolds, James Caan, and Ryan O'Neal. But Stallone, even though he was penniless, gambled that this was his one real shot at stardom. He refused to sell the script without a guarantee that he'd also star in the movie. Eventually, he got someone to bite, and the rest is movie history. The movie was shot for under a million dollars on the streets of Philadelphia.

Once the movie was completed, the producers and Stallone didn't know if they had a success on their hands. That was 1976, and I was a film major at Loyola Marymount University. At the time, I was taking a film criticism class. Each week we would be shown a movie that had not yet been released. We had a chance to listen to and ask questions of someone connected to the film, and then we were required to write essays about what we had learned. I loved that class—it was everything I loved to do, and I actually got college credit for it.

One of our ongoing challenges was to find out what the film would be in advance. The professors tried to keep it a secret, but inevitably word would leak out. One night, as we showed up for class, it would be fair to say that we weren't thrilled about the possibilities. All we knew was that we were going to see a boxing movie starring some guy named Sylvester.

The movie, of course, was *Rocky*. We were the first audience to see a finished print. We had no expectations, no preconceptions. And to say we were blown away would be an understatement.

There's a message in here for business: never underestimate the importance of surprising your customers. I'm not sure how many companies say, "Let's find a way to surprise the customer today." But I think it is always worth doing.

To this day, I cannot ever remember being part of an audience that had such a visceral response to a motion picture. During the climactic fight scene against Apollo Creed, we were all on our feet, cheering and shouting. It might as well have been a real boxing match. When it was over, we all were crying and exhausted and completely enthralled by the experience—and then Sylvester Stallone walked in to take our questions, and the place erupted all over again. This was before he was Stallone the icon. He was a little shy, a little amazed, and completely in the moment.

Rocky made millions, garnered dozens of awards, and went on to spawn a bunch of sequels. And all because this out-of-work actor, propelled by little other than desire, wrote a script about a broken down fighter who was propelled by little other than desire.

I'm not sure this lesson means that every morning when a company opens its doors, the theme from *Rocky* should blare from the loudspeakers.

But it couldn't hurt.

MICHAEL'S POV:

Rocky, and even the weak sequels, always delivered another important lesson to me and that's recognizing weaknesses and working to fix them. When Rocky first gets handed a miracle—a title bout—he approaches it with the same lackadaisical attitude he's approached everything in life. Before getting that fight, he actually gets scolded by his coach for never putting in the hard work needed to achieve his potential. When that same coach offers to train Rocky for the big fight, Rocky rejects him. But then he realizes that without coaching, he won't just lose, he'll get embarrassed. Rocky swallows his pride and starts putting in the hard work (you'll never think of an early morning workout or raw eggs the same way again) and becomes a better fighter. Mentors matter, as does hard work, discipline, and accepting direction from someone who knows better.

"Take Two"

BIOPIC / DOCUMENTARY

Find a Role Model

RB	RULE BREAKERS
E	ETHICS
L	LEADERSHIP

Suggested for all business audiences

THERE ARE RARE TIMES WHEN THE REAL LIFE STORY of an individual is so powerful, so moving, and so compelling, and when a story is so large and important that it takes the most accomplished moviemaker to tell the tale.

Such is the incredible power of two Oscar-winning movies: *Gandhi* and *Schindler's List.* Although the men at the center of both movies lived at the same time, their stories could not be more different. *Gandhi* tells a story of the difference between power and authority; *Schindler's List* demonstrates the ability of a single person to make an amazing difference in a time of insanity. They are movies that everyone should watch both to enjoy the story and to gain inspiration for the potential for greatness that lies in all of us.

If *Gandhi* were a work of fiction, not a biography, the viewer would hardly believe the story is real. In fact, within the first few minutes of the film, in a flashback to Gandhi's funeral, the movie makes that exact point through a newsman reporting on the proceedings:

"And Albert Einstein added, 'Generations to come will scarce believe that such a one as this ever in flesh and blood walked upon this earth.'"

But that is what makes this movie so incredible. *Gandhi*, directed by the legendary Richard Attenborough, tells the story of a very common man who changed the world. The words of the opening scenes tell us what we need to know:

"The object of this massive tribute died as he had always lived...a private man without wealth, without property, without official title or office. Mahatma Gandhi was not a commander of great armies, nor ruler of vast lands. He could boast no scientific achievement, no artistic gift. Yet men, governments, and dignitaries from all over the world have joined hands today to pay homage to this little brown man in the loincloth who led his country to freedom...A man who made humility and simple truth more powerful than empires."

Every scene in this three-hour-long movie lays out the story. Mohandas K. Gandhi was simply a lawyer heading off to South Africa for a job when he ran headlong into a world of injustice. Confronted by South Africa's racial policies and second-class treatment of its Indian citizens, Gandhi is moved to action.

The movie makes it clear that Gandhi is no saint. While he fights for the rights of Indians, we hear no speeches about South Africa's oppressed black majority. And the relationship between Gandhi and his wife is handled delicately throughout the movie as his wife clearly chafes at her husband's ideals.

Gandhi is undeterred by beatings, imprisonment, and other difficulties. We watch him grow as a leader and watch the British colonialists grow increasingly unable to cope with him. By the time he leaves South Africa, his points are won and he's heading home to India. And there we see the development of a legendary leader.

Gandhi leads India from a colony to independence without violence or bloodshed. At one point he promises the British that in the end they will leave India, the crown jewel of all the British colonies, without a single shot. And he lives up to his word, though the process is not without pain and bloodshed.

And here is where Gandhi the man and *Gandhi* the film show us the power of leadership. At no point does Gandhi take an official title or any other sign of power. He leads in the way that only a great leader can: through action, through integrity, and through example. While clearly a master of grand gestures—we witness his famed hunger strikes and walks across the vast subcontinent of India—Gandhi moves with endless humility. Even as his followers take to calling him Mahatma, the "great soul," Gandhi continues to live and preach a simple life.

It's a powerful contrast to business environments where leaders measure their control in perks, office size, and staffing empires. Sometimes, the most profound leaders have none of those weapons. Rather, they lead with integrity, humility, action, and hard work.

Schindler's List tells the story of a very different type of hero. When we first meet Oskar Schindler we see no sign of heroics in him at all. We don't hear about virtue or humility. Instead, we meet a character who, at first glance, is reprehensible. Schindler is a Nazi in Poland and he has a plan to profit from the war by using slave labor from the Jewish population. He drinks, he womanizes, and we see no sign that this will change.

But it does.

After witnessing the round up and murder of Jews in a Nazi raid, Schindler begins to develop a conscience. He starts finding ways to manipulate the system, deceiving German guards and officers as he protects the Jews working at his munitions factory. The Jews begin to notice, too, and slowly make requests of Schindler to help various prisoners. Schindler does help, adding them to his workforce and giving his "Schindler Jews" far better conditions than they would face in the concentration camps.

Schindler's List, directed by Steven Spielberg, reminds us of the reality of the Holocaust. We see an inmate shot for no reason; we see women prick their fingers and spread blood on their cheeks to appear healthy and worthy of life; we see children climb into a septic tank to avoid capture.

The name of the movie comes from a historically accurate event.

With Nazi Germany collapsing and the Soviet Army moving through Poland, Schindler uses bribes to arrange a deal to move his 1,100 Jewish workers toward then-Czechoslovakia. If not on Schindler's list of workers, they face certain death at Auschwitz. Schindler spends his entire fortune keeping his workers alive, while ensuring that his new factory never once produces weapons that are usable by the Nazi army.

When the war is over and Schindler is at last able to set the Jews free, he sobs that he should have found a way to save even more people. He berates himself for not selling more possessions to essentially buy more people for his list. In that same scene, his chief worker (ironically, played by Ben Kingsley, the same actor who portrays Gandhi in *Gandhi*) presents him with a gold ring bearing an inscription that provides a stunning moral and leadership lesson:

"Whoever saves one life saves the entire world."

Few of us will ever face a situation as horrific as the Holocaust, but we will all face crossroads and times when we can act to help or walk away. *Schindler's List* reminds us that there are no small actions because the consequences of what we do are enormous.

KEVIN'S POV:

The conscience can be an inconvenient thing, especially in the business world. Another movie that demonstrates the importance of conscience is Michael Mann's *The Insider*, which tells the true story of Jeffrey Wigand (played by Russell Crowe), a Brown & Williamson tobacco executive who decides to go on *60 Minutes* to expose the tobacco industry's efforts to hide the addictive and toxic nature of cigarettes. In doing so, he puts his life and family at risk—not for the glory, but because it is the right thing to do. One has to wonder why more executives did not feel conscience-driven to fight an industry that was addicting and killing millions of Americans. Was the money just too good? And what happened when their kids started smoking? Were they able to turn off the ethical centers of their brains? Or had they just so bought into the fiction that smoking was harmless that it never occurred to them that they were in ethical quicksand? Hard to imagine…

Ironically, the television producer who provides the outlet for Wigand, Lowell Bergman (Al Pacino), finds that CBS News is in some ways no better than the tobacco companies when they shelve the interview because of corporate pressure. Eventually the story comes out, but the reputation of CBS News is damaged. *The Insider* is the story of what happens when you listen to—or ignore—your conscience. You don't have to be Gandhi or Schindler. Sometimes you just have to be a business executive who wants to do the right thing.

SELENA (1997)

Celebrate Diversity

THERE ARE MANY WAYS TO DIVIDE PEOPLE on planet Earth. One way: people who knew who Selena was and the rest of us.

I had no idea that Selena Quintanilla-Perez was the queen of Tejano music. Then again, I didn't know what Tejano music was. Likewise, I didn't know her albums sold at a pace equaled only by Michael Jackson. Nor did I know that 65,000 people once crowded into the Houston Astrodome to hear her sing.

In fact, I never knew anything about Selena until after she was killed in 1995. And then the only way I knew about her was when I read an article by a newspaper reporter who was equally stunned that someone so famous and so seriously mourned in parts of the United States had died, and so many of us had never heard of her.

There's a powerful lesson in our ignorance. Our society is blessed with diversity in ways we never imagine, but as a consequence, there are many things going on that we never really know about.

Selena is a rare case where the fact of the movie itself teaches us a lesson beyond the script. The movie shows a classic American success story of a first-generation citizen and her family working hard to build an incredible business and wealth beyond their imagination. It happened on stages in front of thousands of people, with albums that garnered awards and rang up huge sales. Yet, it happened in a way that most Americans probably never noticed.

In the United States today, and in many other countries, diversity is a fact. But the once-vaunted melting pot doesn't work as well as it used to. Today we can watch cable stations devoted only to people who have the exact same interests or points of view that we share. Today we go on Internet sites to link with people whom we know through our specialized interests. Even in a newspaper like the *Washington Post* you can find comic strips geared to different parts of the population—young and old, white and black and Hispanic.

The same occurs with movies and television shows. Ratings of top television shows, for instance, vary considerably based on the makeup of their audience.

In short, we often fail to interact with the diversity all around us, which is a dangerous practice for any business. *Selena* helps us see into the world of Hispanic culture, the world of the quickest-growing and largest minority population in the United States. And therefore, it's a culture non-Hispanics must learn more about to succeed as businesspeople or employers in the future.

So who was Selena?

The movie tells the story of the Quintanilla family's struggles in business and their attempt to create a band, which takes off when young Selena, played brilliantly by Jennifer Lopez, emerges as a star. Selena sings Spanish songs to the Mexican-American population in the southwestern U.S., gaining fans and acclaim as she goes. By the age of 16, she has won awards for her albums and her fan base is exploding.

Her story is truly amazing, with her musical and business success growing at every turn. Sadly, her story, her life—and the movie—end when her deranged fan club president shot her to death just before her 24th birthday.

In *Selena*, we see the vibrancy of the Mexican-American culture in the festivals and fairs where her group performs. We get a glimpse into some of the struggles of Mexican-Americans who, as explained by Selena's father, are neither Mexican nor American enough to be accepted by either side. We see the trials of an American family making its way to success.

We see racism when a sales clerk in a posh dress store treats Selena and a friend dismissively. And we watch Selena's subtle revenge minutes later when the store is overrun by fans who recognize the singing star and crowd around her for autographs.

Selena is a lesson about the worlds around us that we don't see because they aren't in *our* world. And it's a worthy reminder that our experiences aren't universal. Success may depend on us knowing about the other cultures that make up our workforce, our customers, our neighborhoods, and our nation.

A fitting reminder of this comes not from *Selena*, but from Selena's real story. Shortly after her death, radio celebrity Howard Stern made a joke about the incredible displays of mourning. Stern, who is well known for his unapologetic insults, soon apologized in Spanish. And the then-governor of Texas, George W. Bush, declared a day in Selena's honor.

Diversity is all around us, and we should pay attention.

Never Underestimate Your Competition

B	BRANDING
RB	RULE BREAKERS
CF	CUSTOMER FOCUS
L	LEADERSHIP
Suggested for all business audiences	

THE AMERICAN ENTREPRENEURIAL SPIRIT is often characterized by a unique sort of almost naïve optimism—think Jimmy Stewart in all those Frank Capra movies, charging forward with hardly a doubt that positive energy, hard work and a good idea will result in success. It is part of our pioneer charm. It also is fair to suggest that in modern-day America there are strong forces at work that involve a different sort of reality: sometimes you can have a great idea, and it doesn't matter. Execution is critically important to business success, but sometimes even great execution doesn't matter. Sometimes, as Dizzy Dean once said, it is better to be lucky than good.

In *Tucker*, the protagonist's luck runs out.

Tucker, directed by Francis Ford Coppola, is the story of Preston Tucker, a real-life entrepreneur who in the late 1940s developed a car that had a lot of things that the typical car then did not have, including disk brakes, seat belts, a pop-out safety windshield, and an independent four-wheel suspension. Now, to be sure, Tucker was eccentric. He was always a little short of money because his plans got ahead of his finances. Tucker pushed ahead with blind faith that a good idea would always come out on top.

Played with Capra-style buoyancy by Jeff Bridges, Tucker is a character who is so wrapped up in his own dreams that he does not pay attention to either the minutiae of running a company, nor to the realities of the marketplace. He knows his car is a smart and innovative idea, but he doesn't really understand the competition or the politics of the real world. Tucker does not realize American automobile companies will see him as a threat to what they view as their well-earned complacency. They persuade a Michigan senator (played with thinly veiled venality by Lloyd Bridges) to throw bureaucratic and legal roadblocks at Tucker as he works to build his car.

The end is not a happy one, despite the fact that Tucker is able to make 50 of his cars. He is charged with stock fraud, but acquitted, and eventually goes into bankruptcy. The real Preston Tucker died of a heart attack just seven years after the time period of the movie, so real life wasn't any kinder to him than reel life. It should be noted, however, that 47 of the original 50 Tucker automobiles continue to function today, more than a half century after they were built.

It's remarkable to see this movie now, at a time when American car companies have lost market share, have gone into bankruptcy, and are struggling to regain a competitive foothold. At one point in the movie an automobile executive denigrates Tucker's efforts, saying, "A well-run corporation doesn't waste money to research innovations, unless, of course, keeping up with the competition demands it." That may explain the problems of the American car business in one sentence.

At some level, that phrase may also be Coppola's opinion of the American movie business. Coppola certainly is one of the most interesting and inventive filmmakers of a generation that gave us, among others, Steven Spielberg and Martin Scorsese. But he has had a famously checkered career. His roster of films includes classics like the first two *Godfather* movies, *The Conversation*, and *Apocalypse Now*, some mainstream Hollywood hits (*The Rainmaker*) and duds (*Jack*), as well as some more stylized films that range from *The Outsiders* to most recently, *Tetro*. If he's never had the consistent commercial success of Spielberg, Coppola still can take some comfort in knowing that he made perhaps the best movie of all time with *The Godfather*; he's certainly flirted with business disaster more often, displaying the kind of survival skills that any business executive would envy.

Not only has he written, directed, and produced movies for more than four decades, but he's also endured bankruptcy, published a literary magazine, and created an enduring legacy with his Northern California vineyards. Except in those cases when he took a movie to generate some needed income—and we all have to make those kinds of reality-based decisions from time to time—Coppola has created a personal brand that is connected to a kind of creative adventurousness. He almost certainly saw a soul mate in Preston Tucker.

So, what are lessons of *Tucker*?

1. The most important ingredient in any business plan is innovation. A really good idea is critical and can offer a differential advantage, though not an unassailable one. But you've got to have the right strategy and tactics in order to implement it. *Tucker* vividly illustrates that innovation only works when layered on a strong business plan and solid management. You need the basics of execution to survive; the flash of innovation to thrive. Preston Tucker had only the second, while the American auto industry stalwarts focused on the first.

2. Know the competition. It is critical to have a clear-minded view of what competitors are capable of, and how the customers that you have in common will view them. A 21st century reality is this: Think about your most feared competitor. Pretend they're moving in across the street from you. Act accordingly. Repeat.

3. It may not have worked for Preston Tucker in the long run, but it is important, whenever possible, to personalize a business. Putting a face on a company or a product, whether it is a movie or wine company, is a way of creating a sense of human integrity that stands behind whatever

the offering might be. If you doubt this, consider your own life as a consumer and whether the establishments you like to patronize the most are the ones that you can connect to a specific person.

I've always thought that the best business model in some ways ought to be a great bartender. When the customer walks through the door, there's an instant connection and even if you're feeling bad, you have to smile. I think about my three favorite places in the U.S. to have a beer or glass of wine—Etta's Seafood in Seattle, Bin 36 in Chicago, and the River Cat Grille in Connecticut—and I know it isn't just the quality of the libations, but the guys behind the bar—Morgan, Jimmy, and Terry—who give those places personality.

That's the power of the human connection.

Shape Perception to Succeed

B	BRANDING
Suggested for all business audiences	

IT'S HARD TO IMAGINE a more unexpected trajectory than the thin line connecting a small budget movie about body builders to the governorship of California.

Yes, Arnold Schwarzenegger's path is nothing if not unusual. However, the lesson he delivered in that long ago documentary probably guides him to this day. It is the lesson of how the competitor who is better prepared can find ways to tilt the odds in his favor.

Pumping Iron documents the strange life of body builders preparing to battle for the title of Mr. Olympia 1975. The competition is, in many respects, a beauty competition, with the contestants working on muscle mass, posing, and even ballet-like moves to help them impress the judges. The preparation is staggering, with long hours and endless stories of the price of dedication.

The back story of the documentary is about Schwarzenegger, who was the five-time defending champion with no plans to seek a sixth title. Having begun to act in small parts in movies, Schwarzenegger was not planning to enter the 1975 competition until the moviemakers sold him on the idea.

But Schwarzenegger had a problem. He wasn't in full-time training and had lost weight, a big problem for a body builder. He had only a few months to get ready for the competition, which was taking place in South Africa.

He had another very big problem: Lou Ferrigno. Ferrigno would gain fame in later years playing the Incredible Hulk in the television series of that name. He was far bigger and better trained than Schwarzenegger. Ferrigno held the advantage going into the competition and had every expectation of winning.

Schwarzenegger had a different idea. Ferrigno might have had the advantage, but Schwarzenegger planned to win the competition before they ever reached the stage. Not by cheating, but simply by destroying the mental toughness, confidence, and attitude that a body builder needs to project to the judges.

Talking to the producers on camera, Schwarzenegger outlined his strategy:

"The day of the contest, if he comes in his best shape and he's equally as good as I am...or if, let's say, he's a few percent better than I am...I spend with him one night. I go downstairs and book us together in a room...to help him for tomorrow's contest. And that night...he will never forget. I will mix him up.

"He will come so ready to South Africa, so strong. But by the time the night is over, the next morning...he will be ready to lose.

"I mean I will just talk him into that; it's no problem to do."

Then we watch the plan in action. One morning at breakfast, Schwarzenegger invites Ferrigno and his father (Ferrigno's coach) to his table and begins work. By the end of the meal, he has the two Ferrignos agreeing that the timing of the competition is just slightly off for the bigger man. Schwarzenegger makes it clear that Ferrigno would easily win if only the competition was taking place just one month later. But, of course, it isn't.

And just like that, Ferrigno's aura is shattered and the title is Schwarzenegger's to win again, which he does.

Now it's easy to say that business competition is different and that one competitor could never simply talk another into defeat. Then again...

Think of how perceptions are formed in the marketplace. Think of how one competitor, with sharp advertising, sharp logistics, and sharp target marketing can completely alter the landscape of a market before even a single competitive shot is fired.

There are countless case studies showing how consumers will quickly name competitor A as having the lowest prices in town, even though competitor B actually has the advantage. Or that competitor C is thought to have significantly better service/variety/quality, while competitor D actually has the upper hand.

But perceptions are formed carefully. Amazon.com has formed an incredible price and value image in customers' minds by highlighting specific product categories. Many of Amazon's products are supplied by other merchants, and very often competitors have lower prices. But the precision of Amazon's marketing strategy allows its customers to believe they are getting the lowest prices, even if they aren't.

Consider why in the early era of video recording, the far superior Beta players lost out to the VHS format. Or why Microsoft operating systems achieved near universal use, despite their technological shortcomings. Perception can often win the game, even if a competitor has a better product.

Pumping Iron puts it in a very easy package to understand. Winning frequently happens before the game is even played.

Just listen to Arnold.

KEVIN'S POV:

Schwarzenegger's entire career is a testament to the power of packaging. Nobody would ever suggest that he's a particularly good actor, but he was canny from almost the very beginning of his Hollywood career about choosing projects that would play to his strengths, not his weaknesses, and would stretch him just enough to insure that audiences wouldn't tire of him. That meant moving from simple action movies like *Terminator* to action movies with comedy like *Kindergarten Cop* to outright comedies like *Twins*. And for a long time, it worked...until, of course, the inevitable expiration date on Hollywood stardom, at which point Schwarzenegger went into politics. It'll be interesting to see what he does next. I'd guess that it will be something that will both play to his strengths and demonstrate a continuing evolution.

That's something we all have to do in our businesses. Keep moving, keep evolving, keep building on our achievements and always, always remember the importance of packaging.

"*Take Three*"

CLASSICS

Business Exists in the Real World

RB	RULE BREAKERS
L	LEADERSHIP

Suggested for all business audiences

IN ADDITION TO BEING ONE OF THE MOST influential films in Hollywood history, *Citizen Kane* is also one of the best business movies ever made. The movie traces the life and career of newspaper mogul Charles Foster Kane. As directed, co-written, and portrayed by Orson Welles, Kane's life is inextricably tied up in his image and power as a media magnate, although the film makes clear he has holdings in grocery stores, gold mines, paper mills, real estate, ocean liners, and assorted other businesses.

In one way, *Citizen Kane* is a classic mystery—the search for the meaning behind Kane's dying word: "Rosebud" (I won't divulge the ending here, though most people, even those who have not seen the movie, know it). The search for the meaning of his last word also is a search for the meaning of Kane's life, which is the business lesson of *Citizen Kane.* Even though he has a declaration of principles printed on the front page of the first paper he decides to run, Kane doesn't really have any core principles—not in his work, and not in his life. Kane's lack of principles leads to the corruption of the man and his work.

That's not to say that Kane does everything wrong. Far from it. When he first goes into the newspaper business, he does it because he thinks, "It would be fun to run a newspaper," which I've always thought is the best reason to get into any business. Work and business take up an enormous percentage of our lives, and if it isn't going to be fun, what's the point?

When Kane publishes his declaration of principles, his best friend, Jed Leland, notes that all the sentences begin with "I." "People are going to know who is responsible," Kane replies, and that's a great lesson for any business. Anonymity at the top has little value. Think of how companies like Chrysler or Perdue or Wendy's were able to build tremendous equity because they were run or founded by visible individuals like Lee Iacocca, Frank Perdue and Dave Thomas. People like to know who is in charge because it creates a sense not only of personality, but of accountability.

Citizen Kane serves as a cautionary tale about mistakes that the people who run businesses can make.

Charles Foster Kane acquires things not out of a strategic vision, but because he likes to acquire. As one character says about him, "He never used his money to invest. He just liked to buy things." That can be a dangerous impulse for a business; if an acquisition does not support the core brand equity, or represent a strategic expansion with integrative value, then it may not make sense, especially now, when the phrase "too big to fail" has taken on such a pejorative meaning.

Kane also is a victim of enormous hubris. He hires away the best writers from a rival newspaper, but as Leland observes, it is by no means certain that Kane will be able to train them to put out his kind of newspaper. It remains entirely possible that they will change him, making him a more traditional publisher and therefore, dilute his differential advantage.

Kane runs for governor, and even when his infidelities are revealed, he believes that the love of the people will be enough to launch him into office and an eventual run for the presidency. But this is the 1920's, and people were far less forgiving then. When his girlfriend expresses an interest in singing, he believes that by giving her lessons and building an opera house, he can turn her into an opera star, which of course, he cannot. On "American Idol," she would have been an early round joke for Simon Cowell.

"He was disappointed in the world, so he built one of his own," one character says about Kane's building of Xanadu, the Florida castle, secluded behind barbed wire and walls and moats, where he spends the latter years of his life among meaningless possessions and in a loveless marriage. Despite the fact that Kane is still in business, he grows increasingly out of touch with the real world and what his customers want. Kane thinks he knows best and that he can mold the world in his image.

For any businessperson, *Citizen Kane* is a wonderful example of how leadership can work, but also how myopic vision can cause an institution to crash because of personal delusions and detachment. Even viewing it now, almost seven decades after it was first released, "Citizen Kane" is a remarkably modern movie—in tone, in context, and in content. It is a must-see for businesspeople looking for narratives to both embrace and avoid.

GUYS AND DOLLS (1955)
TIN CUP (1996)

Don't Take
the Uneducated Risk

RB	**RULE BREAKERS**
	Suggested for all business audiences

ARROGANCE IS A WORD EVERY BUSINESSPERSON should know. It means "excessive pride or self-confidence," according to the dictionary. It's about believing that whenever we jump we're destined to fly, even if gravity has other plans.

Two very, very different movies give us some very, very easy reminders of the natural skepticism we forget when arrogance kicks in. This may be the first time a musical starring Marlon Brando and Frank Sinatra ever ends up referenced alongside a Kevin Costner sports comedy. But these lessons require some new connections.

The musical *Guys and Dolls*, based on two short stories by Damon Runyon, is about New York gamblers always looking for a way to beat the odds. Brando's character Sky Masterson is willing to bet on almost anything, but early in the movie he reveals his philosophy, which happens to be a nugget of caution left to him by his father.

Masterson's father told him, "One of these days, a guy is going to show you a brand-new deck of cards on which the seal is not yet broken. Then this guy is going to offer to bet you that he can make the jack of spades jump out of this brand-new deck of cards and squirt cider in your ear.

"But, son, you do not accept this bet because as sure as you stand there you're going to wind up with an ear full of cider."

In other words, look very carefully before you leap. When Bernie Madoff came calling with his "safe" investment, the consistent returns seemed too good to be true. And they certainly were. It is easy to start believing in our own or someone else's arrogance. Certainly some risks should be taken and opportunities seized, but at any given moment we should remind ourselves of Sky Masterson's story and consider how we could end up with cider in our ear.

Tin Cup provides another example of the danger of forgetting to think through all the details. Costner's character, Roy McAvoy, is a wonderful natural golfer whose complete lack of discipline and focus has condemned him to a life of running a ramshackle driving range. To make matters worse, his college teammate, David Simms (played by Don Johnson), makes it big as a professional golfer with less talent, but copious amounts of, and possibly too much, discipline. The plot revolves around their both pursuing the same love interest, Molly Griswold (Rene Russo).

McAvoy decides the way to get even is to qualify for the U.S. Open and show the world and Griswold who is really the best. Being who he is, McAvoy survives a qualifying match despite breaking all but one of his clubs. When he brags about this, Simms offers him a challenge: who can hit the longest shot with the remaining club? McAvoy gladly accepts and proceeds to hit a remarkably long shot into the golf course.

Unexpectedly, Simms take the same club and turns around to face the road, hitting a shot that bounces endlessly off the paved surface and into the distance, winning the bet.

The message again is simple. Know the competition, know the situation, and take a hard look at all the various ways a scenario can play out. Risks are worth taking, but make them educated risks. Honestly evaluate your own (and your organization's) strengths and weaknesses. And don't go gambling your future and capital without some sense of the unexpected challenges you might face.

Fortune may favor the brave. But common sense and some caution could keep you from wiping cider out of your ear...or worse.

Don't Breathe
Your Own Exhaust

E	ETHICS
RB	RULE BREAKERS

Suggested for all business audiences

YEARS AGO, MICHAEL AND I WERE SPEAKING to a food industry executive about our work on *MorningNewsbeat.com* and some other projects for which we'd been getting positive reviews. He said something very important that day, something we've both tried to keep in mind:

"Don't breathe your own exhaust."

That's very good advice, when you think about it. The simple fact is that most people like to be positive and hate to be negative. So when people give you feedback, they, in the words of the Johnny Mercer song, "accentuate the positive and eliminate the negative."

It's why legendary grocer Stew Leonard always has said that criticism is a lot more important to running a business than compliments, since the people who offer approbations already are fans. Criticism, on the other hand, offers two significant advantages—it gives you the opportunity to improve, and it generally comes from people who feel strongly enough about your business to take the time to complain.

Breathing your own exhaust is akin to only paying attention to the positives, which distracts you from dealing with the negatives, and in the case of two movies, *All About Eve* and *Misery*, diverts attention from serious personnel issues.

Watch your back when people are too complimentary. That's the central message of *All About Eve*, which was written and directed by Joseph L. Mankiewicz and starred Bette Davis and Anne Baxter.

The plot is pretty simple. Margo Channing (Davis) is a famous but aging Broadway star. Eve Harrington (Baxter) is a fan who insinuates herself into Channing's life, becoming her assistant and then her understudy, and eventually tricking Channing into missing a performance so she can go on in her stead. Harrington is every employer's worst nightmare—a scheming, manipulative underling with designs on the boss's job.

All About Eve, of course, is the classic worst-case scenario. Harrington not only does her best to infiltrate Channing's life and career, but she tries to seduce and blackmail her way to the top. All the signs of sabotage are there, but nobody is paying attention. That lack of concern is a symptom of bad management.

The message in *All About Eve* is cautionary. Watch your back. Even the people you trust may have knives at the ready.

Which leads to the second example of the same problem, as demonstrated in the movie *Misery*.

Fans can be dangerous.

Based on the Steven King novel, *Misery* is the story of novelist Paul Sheldon (James Caan), who finds himself at the mercy of Annie Wilkes (Kathy Bates), who has rescued him from a car accident in a blizzard. Annie, who declares herself to be Sheldon's biggest fan, also is a total wingnut—she imprisons Sheldon when she doesn't like the draft of a new novel that he has written, cripples him when he tries to escape, and forces him to write a novel that reflects her own peculiar sensibilities.

Now, to be fair, this isn't really a management problem. Annie doesn't work for Sheldon. But this is a great example of how you cannot—or, at least, should not—believe even your most dedicated enthusiasts, because they may very well have ulterior motives.

Part of management is making sure that the people who work for you have your best interests at heart or at least understand that your best interests are their best interests. I am reminded of the story told by performance strategist Art Turock about Pete Carroll, head football coach at the University of Southern California (USC). Carroll understands that his assistant coaches all have their own career goals. Rather than worry about them leaving USC, he encourages them to be vocal about their aspirations and even runs mock sessions so they can get practice at job interviewing.

"How many companies pay that kind of attention to the goals and dreams of their employees?" Turock asks. Not many, I would answer. And I'm guessing that Carroll gets people lining up to work for him since it is well established that he is interested in their advancement.

Benjamin Zander, conductor at the Boston Philharmonic Orchestra, speaks eloquently of his realization that the conductor is the only member of the orchestra who does not make a sound, but it is the conductor who is primarily responsible for the music created by the ensemble. The only way for a conductor to succeed, says Zander, is to empower his musicians. Zander says part of his success has come from taking a more nurturing rather than autocratic stance with his musicians. The equivalent philosophy in the business world is creating an environment in which people can and want to excel—where they understand that they are part of a whole that sounds much better than each individual instrument.

There's an enormous distance between the place where Margo Channing and Paul Sheldon find themselves and the cultures being created by the likes of Pete Carroll and Ben Zander. It has to do with awareness, understanding that one's own interests often are best served by a level of selflessness.

Don't breathe your own exhaust. That's a sure way to commit business suicide.

THE CAINE MUTINY (1954)
MISTER ROBERTS (1955)

Make the Best
of a Bad Boss

L	LEADERSHIP
RB	**RULE BREAKERS**
Suggested for all business audiences	

THE IMPACT OF THE BAD BOSS—mean, incompetent, controlling, uncaring—can be disastrous for a business. What's more, we remember bad bosses for years, reciting tales of woe to people who have no connection to the actual events.

It's hard to imagine a less flexible situation for dealing with a bad boss than being on a naval vessel in the middle of a war. Two very good yet different lessons about bad bosses come to us from World War II-era movies about the U.S. Navy: a classic comedy, *Mister Roberts*, and a classic drama, *The Caine Mutiny*.

Both stories feature a similar background: the very real leadership problem that hit the U.S. military in World War II. Plunged into war almost overnight by the attack at Pearl Harbor, the military was forced to rapidly staff up to harness sufficient firepower for both the Atlantic and Pacific theaters. While the draft supplied an ample fighting force, trained officers were frequently in short supply.

Both war movies build on this leadership challenge. In *Mister Roberts*, James Cagney plays Captain Morton, looking to move up the ranks, but short of any management skills. His qualification for leadership was his experience in the Merchant Marines. Throughout the movie he seems unable to manage anything.

Henry Fonda plays the title character in *Mister Roberts*, a college-educated executive officer in charge of the cargo ship on a day-to-day basis. Roberts is winning the devotion and support of his troops and battling Morton for control of the ship. Roberts successfully runs the ship, but is undone by two issues. The first is his devotion to his men, which forces him to make deals with his superior, Morton, to win better conditions for the men. The second is his desire to gain transfer to a ship with a chance to see actual combat.

In truth, Roberts never really does solve the problem of Morton being a difficult superior officer. He just works around it. He treats his enlisted men with respect and caring and they return the favor, despite the main plot device that briefly challenges this relationship. Roberts demonstrates that even in the worst of circumstances, a good manager can overcome all the challenges around him by knowing what's most important and keeping his team focused on that goal.

In contrast, Morton never once gets that message, choosing instead a dictatorial style that constantly moves him further from his team. Morton may be the captain, but Roberts runs the ship. What's more, Roberts performs one of the hardest duties of middle management: shielding his direct reports whenever possible from the captain. While he shares his frustrations with his fellow officers, he maintains the chain of command and professionalism in front of his troops.

The management challenge in *The Caine Mutiny* is substantially more complex, more common, and far more difficult to deal with. Humphrey Bogart's portrayal of Captain Queeg paints a picture of another embattled boss, but one whose actions endanger the well-being of his sailors. In situation after situation, he makes faulty decisions that threaten his crew and the battle strategy. Faced with a captain who is clearly incapable of exercising command, the executive staff of the Caine chooses what they see as the only course open to them: they seize control of the ship.

In its final scenes, *The Caine Mutiny* gives its clearest management lesson, in the form of a scolding of the now vindicated executive staff, which includes Van Johnson and Fred MacMurray in excellent performances.

The officers are told by the defense attorney who has won their freedom (Jose Ferrer) that despite their victory in the naval court, they failed. Asked to reflect back on their relationship with Captain Queeg, they recognize that he had reached out to them, albeit in clumsy fashion, for help in running the ship. It may have been very hard for him to admit weakness and ask for help, but Queeg, the bad boss, did it.

And the executive officers simply sat mute. Instead of rallying for the team and possibly improving a difficult situation, they allowed their dislike of Queeg to fester and blow up into a full-scale mutiny. As the movie makes clear, at least one junior officer seemed intent on pushing the situation to full-blown crisis and, in essence, he became the linchpin of the poor relationship.

Employees must exercise innovative thinking to work with bad bosses. In *Mister Roberts,* Fonda's actions allowed his ship to operate efficiently despite the captain. Although the ship was merely a cargo vessel, wars are won and lost in logistics, such as getting necessary supplies to the troops. Mr. Roberts's efforts enabled his ship to operate at strong levels to meet the demands upon them, helping the U.S. win the war in the Pacific.

In contrast, the lack of action by the crew of the Caine produced the opposite effect. A battle vessel, the Caine was supposed to provide support to landing teams in the midst of pitched battles. But handicapped by Queeg's inability to make good decisions and the executive staff's lack of support, the Caine fails repeatedly at its missions.

Sure, a bad boss is a huge problem. In fact, a bad boss can ruin companies, ruin careers and ruin lives. There's no escaping them in the movies, the military or any part of the economy. Figuring out how to manage a bad boss is every bit as important as managing subordinates.

Having a bad boss is no excuse for being a bad employee.

HIGH NOON (1952)
APPALOOSA (2008)

Do the Right Thing

E	**ETHICS**
Suggested for all business audiences	

I LOVE WESTERNS. ALWAYS HAVE. Give me a movie with a horse in it, and I'm pretty much there.

Westerns have not flourished in recent years. They tend not to make a lot of money and are an anachronism in Hollywood.

If westerns are out of fashion, I suspect, it is because they tend to share a certain view of the world that isn't very modern. The ones I like most are about men struggling to find the center, the ethical core of their existence. That may sound pretty fancy, and certainly no self-respecting cowboy would think of it that way, but that's the essence of a great western. A man—sometimes, but not always, the sheriff—looks to impose or represent an ethical sensibility in a town or situation where he has moral, if not necessarily legal, responsibilities.

It's simple. He's trying to do the right thing. He's trying to make sure that the civilization for which he bears some responsibility operates the way it should. He's standing up, often on a lonely, wind-blown, sagebrush-strewn street, when others will not. He's saying the things that need to be said, asking the questions that need to be asked, doing the things that need to be done.

This is not an ethic that we see much in business today, where the headlines have screamed at us over the past few years about people behaving in shady and illegal ways, concerned only about themselves and their own pocketbooks or pleasures without any sense of moral or legal responsibility.

Think about the hedge fund operators or stockbrokers or financial services companies where the concern was not about the customer, but about how many commissions could be churned through constant, even questionable activity. Think about the politicians who talk about family values and yet wander off the marital reservation when lust beckons.

In many westerns, one can see the ancestors of these types of people, who thrive on the belief that they are too big to be challenged, too powerful to be questioned, too rich to be brought down.

A great version of this story is a modern western, *Appaloosa*. Virgil Cole (Ed Harris) and Everett Hitch (Viggo Mortensen) are hired to be the law in the town of Appaloosa, a place where ranch owner Randall Bragg has pretty much done what he wanted to do for as long as anyone can remember, including murder the last marshal. Only Cole and Hitch seem to have the moral certitude, and the talent with weapons, to challenge Bragg's dominance.

There's a wonderful moment when Bragg says to Cole, "I told you you'd never hang me." And Cole responds: "Never ain't here yet." It captures the resoluteness of a person certain he knows what he has to do.

Of course, the granddaddy of this approach to the western is the great classic *High Noon*. Gary Cooper plays Will Kane, a western marshal who has decided to retire from his job, get married (to a Quaker woman, played by Grace Kelly, who does not approve of violence), and become a storekeeper. But when he learns that Frank Miller, a man he sent to jail for murder, has been pardoned and is returning to town on the noon train, he realizes that he has a moral duty to stay and defend the town from the vengeful outlaw. The problem is, nobody wants to help him. Even though he has risked his life defending them for many years, the townsfolk lack the moral backbone to do the same for him. In fact, they are perfectly happy to sacrifice him if it keeps the rest of them safe.

Kane has a choice. He can leave, or he can fight. But the film suggests he really doesn't have a choice. He is compelled by his own strength of character to see justice done or die trying, even if the people he is defending don't deserve it. "I got to," he says. "That's the whole thing."

Simple as that.

Watching a movie like *High Noon* or *Appaloosa* is a great way to begin a conversation within a company about the role of ethical behavior in business—a discussion often not held until it is too late. As Robert B. Parker, author of the bestselling novel on which *Appaloosa* is based, wrote, "Most people don't have much trouble seeing what's right or wrong. Doing it sometimes is complicated, but knowing the right thing is usually not so hard."

Do your people know that your company is committed to ethical practices, to not cutting corners, to doing the right thing even if there is a price to pay? Before you say yes, think hard. Then ask yourself if you have created a culture that would support them or shun them.

And if the answer is the latter, then fix it. Because a man's gotta do what a man's gotta do. Even if the man happens to be a woman.

Stick to the Fundamentals

E	ETHICS
P	PLANNING
Suggested for all business audiences	

IN THE LISTS RANKING THE BEST American movies ever, *Citizen Kane* and *The Godfather* are often above *Casablanca*, in part because they have grand themes in mind, and effectively use art to portray and comment upon human frailties on a large and vivid canvas. But *Casablanca* may in some ways be the more perfect movie, in part because it delivers such a big punch on a modest scale. It is like a small but exquisitely formed diamond, with a wonderful cast, evocative script, and taut direction that keeps the plot moving relentlessly forward.

Businessmen are the main protagonists of all three films: *Citizen Kane* has the media mogul Charles Foster Kane; *The Godfather* has Vito Corleone and Michael Corleone, both of whom are involved in, shall we say, the family business. And *Casablanca* has Rick Blaine, unforgettably played by Humphrey Bogart as a bitter expatriate saloonkeeper in pre–World War II Northern Africa.

Unlike the other two, however, Rick is not defined by his job—in fact, he has turned to running Rick's Café Américain as a way to escape from his past. He has found himself too many times on losing sides, including his brief romance with Ilsa Lund, played by Ingrid Bergman, who was never lovelier or more luminous than in this movie.

Despite a gruff exterior, Rick's essential decency comes through in the way he runs the saloon and especially how he deals with his employees. Some examples:

- When competing saloon owner Ferrari (Sidney Greenstreet) wants him to either sell the bar or the services of Sam the piano player (Dooley Wilson), Rick quickly points out that he does not presume to make decisions for Sam. To prove the point, he goes to Sam and tells him that Ferrari would double his pay. Sam, of course, doesn't even think about it. His loyalty is to Rick.

- When his croupier tells Rick with a degree of concern that one of the patrons has won 20,000 francs, Rick is reassuring and tells him not to worry about it—it is a casino, after all, and losses are to be expected. Rick shows far less hostility to his employees than he does to his customers, some of whom are the focus of his contempt.

- Later in the film, when Captain Renault (Claude Rains), under pressure from the Nazis, shuts down Rick's saloon, Rick decides to keep all his employees on full salary as long as possible. Compare that to all the companies that have used the recent recession as an excuse to cull their ranks and get rid of employees.

- When Rick decides to sell his saloon to Ferrari because his life is about to take an unexpected turn, Rick says that Sam gets 25 percent of the profits. Ferrari says he knows that Sam actually gets ten percent, but he agrees to the larger percentage because he knows that Sam will provide a level of continuity that will keep the bar profitable.

In all these cases, Rick demonstrates a central tenet of good leadership: If you put the employees first, they'll do their best to put the customers first. And that makes for a winning business formula.

There are other business jewels in *Casablanca*. The classic line, "Round up the usual suspects," is an approach to management that businesses should avoid. In the film, it is used for the by-rote approach taken by the police whenever a crime is committed or suspected, resulting in the capture of none of the actual criminals. In business, we have to avoid the "usual suspects," because that reflects closed-minded thinking that cannot generate differentiated results.

Rick assiduously avoids being drawn into political controversies. I couldn't help but be reminded of the small firestorm that Whole Foods CEO John Mackey created when he did the opposite, penning a *Wall Street Journal* editorial criticizing the Obama administration's plans for health care reform and effectively annoying many of the liberals/ progressives who were part of his core customer base. Rick's model avoids alienating the shopper.

I used to work in a clothing store where the owner, Richard Coulter, would post any community-oriented signs or flyers on the front door, except for those that were political in nature. "I don't want to annoy half my customers," he used to say. "And if you get political, that almost certainly is going to happen."

This isn't to suggest that Rick is the perfect businessman. In many ways his cynicism and bitterness—"I stick my neck out for nobody"— may not be the best policy, especially when put into the context of a 21st century business environment where so many customers want to know not just about the value that businesses offer, but also the values that these companies represent. Mackey's mistake may have been that he acted as if he was oblivious to the values held by a strong segment of his customer base.

As *Casablanca* moves toward its inexorably romantic conclusion, we see Rick modify his behavior. He allows a couple to win enough at roulette that they will be able to purchase exit visas and escape Casablanca for America. And he comes to the realization that his self-pity must come to an end—that his own problems "don't amount to a hill of beans" compared to those of the real world.

That's what I call contextual thinking, which is an essential, even fundamental, part of effective business leadership and management.

And as we know, in business as well as the movies, the fundamental things apply…as time goes by.

MICHAEL'S POV:

I see two additional teaching moments in this giant of a film. The first is when Victor Laszlo commandeers the band at Rick's and leads an emotional playing of "La Marseillaise," the French national anthem. Watch the faces of the patrons and get a sense of how an impassioned leader can take command and inspire.

The second scene is a stunning reminder of how quickly circumstances change. In one short exchange with Sam, Rick muses on what's happening in New York at that very moment. The timing of the scene is December 1941 and Rick says, "I bet they're asleep in New York. I bet they're asleep all over America." As everyone knows, the pre-war sleep in America didn't last long. The sneak attack on Pearl Harbor is about to happen. In business or warfare, it's critical to pay attention to the perils of the future at home and around the world.

THE BRIDGE ON THE RIVER KWAI (1957)
JURASSIC PARK (1993)

Understand the Consequences of Your Actions

E	ETHICS
L	LEADERSHIP
Suggested for all business audiences	

MANY YEARS FROM NOW, business historians will examine the calamitous events of 2008 and will struggle to understand what caused the global economic crash. They will have to face the question: How did so many make such a series of ill-considered and wrong-headed decisions?

There are two movies that can help us understand what happened in 2008: the stunning dinosaur movie *Jurassic Park* and the absorbing World War II movie, *The Bridge on the River Kwai.*

Marianne Jennings, a law professor at Arizona State University and a brilliant speaker on business ethics, says *Jurassic Park* talks about a simple notion of ethical behavior that everyone needs to consider. Early in the movie, before the dinosaurs start killing their human "hosts," the park's founder explains how he reanimated the extinct species.

One of his visitors, Ian Malcolm, played by Jeff Goldblum, explains the faulty foundation of the entire effort. As Malcolm puts it, the park's founders asked themselves if they *could* bring the dinosaurs to life, but never once considered if they *should*. That simple question, Professor Jennings explains, could prevent countless ethical breaches. There are many projects and efforts that businesses and individuals undertake because they can, but not because they should. One can only imagine how different history itself would be if this simple question were considered.

How is it that well-meaning people make so many ethical mistakes? Are they malevolent? Or do they simply set off on the wrong path and forget what it is they are doing?

The Bridge on the River Kwai examines decisions gone wrong. The story takes place in a brutal prisoner of war camp in southern Asia during World War II. The detainees are abused and misused by their Japanese captors and rebel constantly. The prisoners, through their non-cooperation, ensure that the Japanese goal of building a railroad bridge over the Kwai is a repeated failure.

The prisoners are punished for their rebellion with malnourishment and solitary confinement in a hot box under the broiling tropical sun.

This cycle of retribution breaks when the British officers suggest to the Japanese that the soldiers might work better if their treatment were better and if they are allowed to work under the leadership of their own officers. The Japanese commandant, desperate to complete the bridge, agrees.

The plan works. The lead British officer, Colonel Nicholson, played by Alec Guinness, takes to the project with diligence. He pushes his soldiers to build the bridge. In one scene, he even walks into the infirmary and conscripts many of the ill to join the construction effort. The project moves forward with efficiency, and the British complete the bridge on schedule. And therein lies the problem.

As the project speeds to completion, many of the British begin to question why they are completing a task for their enemy, building a bridge that will help the Japanese speed soldiers, weaponry, ammunition, and supplies to troops that are killing other allied soldiers. Nicholson won't hear of it. To him, the project has become an obsession and a source of honor for the British.

Nicholson rallied his troops to excellence, but the completed project was a boon for his enemy. He employed his substantial skills for the wrong cause.

There are parallels in the Colonel's behavior to the financial crisis of 2008. The federal government and some financial institutions spurred the development of complex financial instruments that initially were created to make houses affordable for more people. Although there were many rotten apples in the financial world, many efforts to lower the cost of mortgages started with good intentions. But the result of these efforts was that greed and risk made the enterprise a disaster.

Just like Colonel Nicholson in *The Bridge on the River Kwai*, no one stopped to think about what they were really building.

At the end of the film, Nicholson finally sees what has happened, when he almost prevents the destruction of his bridge by his allies. He realizes that in his zeal for the project, he forgot what he was fighting for. His dying words are "What have I done?"

It is a startling moment of realization and one, sadly, that we have not seen displayed by any of the business leaders involved in the myriad scandals. Rather, the only regret we seem to witness is their disappointment at getting caught.

But we have to hope others can and will learn from the lessons of *The Bridge on the River Kwai*. Maybe the next generation of business leaders can grow to understand that sometimes they have to question whether their short-term actions can wipe out a greater good.

"Take Four"

COMEDY

Be Different

THERE IS A PHRASE THAT SHOULD NEVER BE UTTERED in business. It consists of the seven forbidden words:

"That's the way we've always done it!"

You know you have heard the phrase and it is possible that you have even said it. The cumulative impact of the phrase is a non-stop assault on creativity, innovation, and rule breaking—the very activities virtually every company should encourage.

There is a cure for this unbridled corporate conservatism in the form of the delightful movie *Babe*. Every time the phrase *"That's the way we've always done it!"* is uttered, force that person to watch *Babe*. In fact, watch it yourself. It's worth it.

On the surface, *Babe* appears to be a child's movie. It isn't, although it is great for children, too. It's the story of a pig, Babe, who is the runt of the litter destined for the slaughterhouse. Babe is saved from this fate when he is given to a local fair to be handed out as a prize, which is won by taciturn farmer Arthur Hoggett, wonderfully played by James Cromwell.

Once at Hoggett's farm, Babe does something unusual: he stops behaving like a pig, for the simple reason that he doesn't know he's a pig. He consorts with all manner of animals like Ma the old sheep, Ferdinand the duck, and the litter of sheepdogs living in the barn. With his polite manners and naïve ways, Babe becomes a friend to all the animals, many of whom do not get along and clearly do not respect each other. (Hmmm, sounds more like an office with each passing moment.)

Farmer Hoggett begins to notice Babe's social abilities when Babe divides all the chickens in the yard into groups of similar colors. Soon, Farmer Hoggett gives Babe a chance to show his stuff at the most important animal job on the farm, herding the sheep.

That's where Babe the pig and *Babe* the movie shine. By breaking all the rules—"the way things are," as the animals remind him—Babe becomes an outstanding herder. Although the dogs consider the sheep too dumb to understand anything other than a nasty approach and the sheep consider the dogs too stupid to talk with, Babe bridges the divide with friendship and manners. Slowly but surely, even the most reluctant animals begin to understand the wisdom of Babe.

Babe is a simple story, but it contains an important lesson. Think of how many businesses have stuck to the way things always are and completely missed the opportunity to become something entirely new, bigger, and better. Some have taken those opportunities:

- MTV didn't invent video or records, but pulled them together into an entirely new cable channel. CBS, in contrast, owned a television network and a record company, but missed the chance.
- Barack Obama did not discover social networking, but his advanced use of the concept of Internet connections helped his fundraising and campaigning. John McCain's presence on YouTube or Facebook was a fraction of Obama's.
- Google wasn't the first company to offer a search engine for the Internet, but its speed and efficiency helped create a cyberspace dynamo that dwarfs AltaVista, Yahoo, or even Microsoft.

MTV, the Obama campaign, and Google all had their *Babe* moments. They ignored "the way things are always done" and built astounding success by identifying possibilities and filling them with a value proposition that viewers, listeners, and shoppers learned to love.

Babe connects on many levels. The parallel of animal and human behavior has been shown often in the movies, from *Charlotte's Web* to *Animal Farm*. But *Babe* delivered a winning story told in a creative style and with a lesson that could stand the test of time. In fact, the movie was nominated for the Academy Award for Best Picture, an uncommon honor for a "children's" movie.

Be on the lookout for those seven deadly words of business, those seven words that limit your horizons and suck the creativity and spirit out of your people. When someone says, "*That's the way we've always done it!*" launch a counter-attack with the story of a pig that refused to accept things the way they were.

In Tough Times, Quality Wins

L	LEADERSHIP
	Suggested for all business audiences

IN THE MIDST OF THE MARKET MELTDOWN of 2008, my financial advisor gave me the good news and the bad news. The bad news: my portfolio lost nearly 19% of its value in just six weeks. The good news: its performance was significantly better than the market as a whole. Somehow, I felt less than pleased.

Despite my losses, my financial advisor may have performed well. Sailing into headwinds is a difficult assignment, but it is necessary for business survival. The simple truth that most businesses regularly forget is that in good times, everyone is a genius. In good times, sales and profits sometimes grow despite the lack of a great strategy and excellent follow through. In good times, the rising tide actually can lift all boats, including some that aren't the best built.

In tough times, quality wins. In tough times, the mettle of individuals and companies get tested and frequently the strong get even stronger.

A League of Their Own, a wonderful movie about a short-lived women's baseball league experiment during World War II, tells this survival story with amazing clarity.

Too many people have seen this popular movie and missed the lesson entirely.

Ask most people to quote a line from *A League of Their Own* and they'll all repeat the same phrase: "There's no crying in baseball." It's a great line that neatly sums up the challenges the women players faced from their managers, fans, and even family. However, our lesson lies elsewhere.

The story, based on a book written by real members of the All American Girls Professional Baseball League, follows the Rockford Peaches and its strong roster of players. Geena Davis plays star player Dottie Hinson with teammates including Madonna and Rosie O'Donnell in acting turns that nicely fit their well-known off-screen personas.

The plot focuses on Hinson's relationships with her hotheaded sister, who is a pitcher on the team, and with the alcoholic manager of the team, Jimmy Dugan, played by Tom Hanks. A former major league player who is now unhappily saddled with a team of women, Dugan and Hinson form a bond that produces the film's business lesson.

Near the end of the film, Hinson is facing a host of issues. She and her sister have been separated acrimoniously when her sister is moved to a new team; her wounded husband is home unexpectedly from the war; her team is just about to start the playoffs.

Hinson decides to quit the team and return home with her husband. Dugan confronts her demanding to know why. Hinson's response tells it all: "It just got too hard."

Dugan then lets loose his retort, and it's one we should all repeat daily. "It's supposed to be hard. If it weren't hard, everyone would do it. It's the hard that makes it great."

What separates one company from another is *the hard*. What separates excellence in leadership, performance, strategy, and execution from mediocrity is *the hard*. If business success were easy, everyone would achieve it.

That's why the best players, managers, and owners usually win in the long run.

Ask yourself what seems too hard in your business. What challenges could you take, what changes could you make, that would result in a stunning improvement for you, your business, and even your life? The odds are you know exactly what those changes are, but the steps are just too hard. The steps are left untaken and the problem goes on.

For athletes, the hard part is improving their skills and working more than everyone around them to achieve greatness. For businesses, there is the same need for continuous improvement through investments in emerging technologies, facilities, and, of course, people. In tough times, spending money may seem too hard, but that's exactly the point. It's the hard that makes it great and that's what drives companies to success.

Here's another truth: one of your competitors will make that effort. And while you and your business might survive, you will be left behind. Then one day, the tough times come and someone else will win.

Just remember that there's no crying in baseball...or in business.

Be the Customer

CF	**CUSTOMER FOCUS**
	Suggested for all business audiences

BIG IS ABOUT 13-YEAR-OLD JOSH BASKIN, frustrated with the limitations of his age, who is magically transformed into an older version of himself, played by Tom Hanks at his most winning. The new, older Josh moves from New Jersey to New York City, where he finds a job working in the headquarters of a toy company staffed mostly, it seems, by stuffed-shirt executives (played by John Heard and Elizabeth Perkins) who are more interested in spread sheets and marketing reports than they are in their target customers.

But Josh actually **is** part of their target market—he's a 13-year-old boy in the body of a 30-year-old. Josh thrives in the work environment because he understands what kids find appealing and what they find annoying, and he's able to turn that intimate knowledge into a product line that sells. He gets a promotion. He's so successful that he actually begins to melt the heart of Perkins's character, even though it is a relationship that can't possibly work. (Credit the film, by the way, for getting this relationship absolutely right...not just the yearnings, but also the confusion.) Josh's success isn't seen in such benign terms by Heard's character, however, who

91

has lost touch with the whole notion of toys and games and decides to teach Josh a lesson on the racquetball court.

Perhaps the best scene in the movie—and the one that everybody remembers—shows Josh hanging around FAO Schwarz on a Saturday afternoon, totally captivated with the magic of the toy store. He bumps into his company president, MacMillan, played by the great Robert Loggia. Josh starts fooling around with an enormous piano keyboard, and MacMillan can't help himself. He has to join in, and suddenly the two find themselves playing "Heart and Soul" and "Chopsticks." The moment is delightful and illustrates vividly the importance of getting into the customer's head and heart.

One of my major complaints about the food retailing business is that it is charged with selling primarily to women, and yet the people at the top of almost every company are middle-aged men, many of whom don't have any huge love for food and don't particularly like shopping. They don't represent the people to whom they are selling products. This has changed somewhat in the food manufacturing business, with companies like PepsiCo, Kraft, and Sara Lee recently headed by women. But the number of food retailers led by women still is an exceedingly short one, and few of the top 50 U.S. food retailers have a woman in the CEO office.

I'm not suggesting that there needs to be a large-scale firing of all middle-aged men running companies in food retailing. But I do think that we all have to be aware of our limitations and the extent to which we do not represent the customers to whom we are trying to appeal.

That's the business lesson of *Big*. It isn't enough to simply read about customers in research reports. You have to listen, you have to understand, and you have to recognize the limitations of your own perspective. You have to *be* the customer.

MICHAEL'S POV:

Big points out a problem too many companies have: they forget what business they are in. When Josh joins the toy company he meets people who seem to have everything on their mind except making toys.

That's a surefire way to ruin a business. Companies need to remind associates about their key business and core customer every day to build a culture of focus and dedication. Take a look at the corporate executive webpage at PetSmart, for instance: every executive is holding a pet. That's focus. MacMillan Toys is lacking that focus until Josh brings it back. Don't let it happen at your company.

THE PRODUCERS (1968)

Vision Trumps All

RB	RULE BREAKERS
L	LEADERSHIP
P	PLANNING
Suggested for all business audiences	

When planning and execution go hand in hand, they are important components of business success. Larry Bossidy and Ram Charan wrote a wonderful book about this process titled *Execution: The Discipline of Getting Things Done*. But when a solid strategy combines with misguided execution, it usually creates a failure. Companies lose sight of exactly what they are trying to achieve and fail to notice when the process goes off the rails.

We find a splendid example of a well-planned disaster in one of the funniest movies ever created, Mel Brooks's *The Producers*.

The movie itself is an incredible story. Starring Zero Mostel and a young Gene Wilder, it was a very modest box office performer upon its original release. Years later it was turned into a Broadway musical and became a worldwide smash hit, performing far better than the original movie.

But the original 1968 film remains a gem and makes for a wonderful viewing.

The Producers is actually a business story, cast as a farce. It offers a lesson that cannot be ignored: a great plan poorly executed brings horrible results.

The story begins when a mousy Leo Bloom (Wilder) shows up to audit the books of the extraordinarily unsuccessful Broadway producer Max Bialystock (Mostel). Bloom discovers something incredible. In Bialystock's most recent flop, the producer actually raised slightly more money than the play cost to produce. Bialystock begs Bloom to find a way to make the mistake go away.

But Bloom hits on something bigger. Theoretically, a flop could make far more money than a success if the producer sold more than 100 percent worth of shares in the production. After all, in a flop, the show's backers never expect to make or recoup their money, so the producer could walk away wealthy. It's theoretical for Bloom; it's sheer genius for Bialystock.

After much cajoling, the producer convinces the accountant to join him in the scheme and they set out to find the worst possible play ever written to ensure a complete failure. Bialystock and Bloom sift through stacks of manuscripts until Bialystock announces he has found it, a play so bad that it is guaranteed to close early.

The play is titled, "Springtime for Hitler, a gay romp with Adolph and Eva in Berchtesgarten." Clearly, it's a play that wouldn't work in 1960s New York or any other time or place. Armed with the worst play ever, they set out on a comical series of business dealings to hire the world's worst director, worst cast, and to gain the play's rights from the author, a barely disguised Nazi living in New York.

Bialystock sets off to romance the bevy of "little old ladies" who finance his shows. Every scene is hilarious.

But here's where our business lesson comes into sharp view. The plan is straightforward, the goal is simple, and the execution seems flawless. Even though Bialystock seems overwhelmed by his good fortune, no one loses focus on the result. Except no one ever contemplates how the entire formula is coming together.

Clearly, the show is a nightmare. Its opening song, "Springtime for Hitler," even includes dancing SS storm troopers forming the shape of a swastika. The show is so offensive as to guarantee failure. The director is so off base in everything he does, he seems certain to fail. And the actors, especially Dick Shawn as Hitler, are a hilarious mess.

But mixed together, the team produces a comic effect that stuns the audience. As one theatergoer says during intermission, "I never in a million years thought I would love a show called 'Springtime for Hitler.'" The show is a hit and the critics predict it is headed for a lengthy and profitable run, which in the normal world of Broadway is great news. In this case, the backers cannot be paid off, which means Bialystock and Bloom are headed for jail. Of course, they manage even that comically.

The business lesson is clear: the best plan comes apart without attention to execution. Bialystock should have been able to see that once all the elements of his plans combined, they created comedy, not the insult he planned.

Too often project leaders, executives, and CEOs get so focused on the plan that they lose sight of what they are trying to achieve. Years ago, I heard a presentation from a major consumer packaged goods manufacturer explaining how his company produced so many products that failed so quickly. It was simple, he said. The project team never stops to think if anyone would buy the product. They only worry about their budgets, projections and deadlines. The big picture goes out of focus and the little picture runs off the track.

One of the most famous business missteps of all time falls right into this model. In the mid-1980s, Coca-Cola made a stunning decision to alter the flavor of the time-honored beverage. Coke's leadership at the time probably thought, like Bialystock and Bloom, that they had a foolproof idea. Consumer tastes were changing and every test Coke did on the new product—a sweeter version of the soft drink—showed it was destined to be a success. They had a strategy and they started executing.

Only Coke misread the messages or lost touch somehow with the bigger picture. As it turned out, when people bought Coke they were buying more than a soft drink; they were buying a memory, a standard, and an experience they couldn't easily change. Overnight sales of New

Coke, the better tasting product, started plummeting and rival Pepsi started crowing.

Coke quickly realized the mistake, brought back the old recipe and rebuilt Coke Classic into a powerhouse again. The recovery was a brilliant rebound by the Coca-Cola marketing machine, but it wasn't a formula that many companies can replicate.

More than 80 percent of the new products introduced in any given year don't survive to their second year. Success is a matter of planning, yes, but also of keeping focus all the way through the execution of the plan. And it's also a matter of understanding that sometimes plans need to be revisited, adjusted, and possibly abandoned all together.

Only in *The Producers* could all these mistakes produce a success. In real life, tragedy, not comedy, is usually the result.

KEVIN'S POV:

A further business lesson can be gleaned from the history of *The Producers*. One of the reasons that the Broadway musical (which I saw four times) works so well is that it takes the basic premise of the original movie and extrapolates on it, making an old story utterly original. Brooks brought in a co-writer, Thomas Meehan, and a director, Susan Stroman, who gave his concept juice.

However, when it came time to make the new film version of the musical version of the original movie, it seemed like all the juice had dried up. There was no joy in it, no sense of discovery. Maybe it was because they stayed too close to the stage version, which didn't transfer well to film; maybe they just went to the well one too many times. Whatever the reason, *The Producers* ended with a whimper, not a bang. Which is a business lesson in and of itself.

THE WEDDING SINGER (1998)
50 FIRST DATES (2004)

Romance Your Customers

RB	RULE BREAKERS
CF	CUSTOMER FOCUS
Suggested for all business audiences	

AT FIRST GLANCE, FINDING A USEFUL BUSINESS LESSON from the movies of Adam Sandler is, in the words of one famed Meat Loaf song, like "looking for a ruby in a pile of rocks." It's just not likely. But a little effort can lead to some gems of advice.

In *Mr. Deeds*, Sandler reminds us of the importance of honesty and integrity in business even in the face of relentless pressure to do otherwise.

In *Waterboy, Billy Madison, Big Daddy, Happy Gilmore,* or…well, let's not push the model too far.

Then there's *The Wedding Singer* and *50 First Dates.* The former provides a classic example on communication and the latter a stunning reminder of the essence of good customer service.

Let's start with *The Wedding Singer.* In the movie, Sandler plays Robbie Hart, a wedding singer whose own wedding is destroyed when his fiancée leaves him standing at the altar. The following day, Robbie, to his shock, is visited at home by his erstwhile love. She shocks him further by informing him that as she reflected on the wedding she just destroyed, she realized she couldn't possibly marry him in part because he worked as a wedding singer.

Robbie looks at her in disbelief and then half-screams the key line: "Another thing you could have told me YESTERDAY!"

He's right. Not wanting to marry him was one thing, but keeping the reason for her refusal a secret caused him added humiliation and, no doubt, a significant amount of cost.

Many of us have been in situations at work when an entire presentation, project, proposal, or meeting is completely undermined because a key piece of information is missing. Even more infuriating is when one of our co-workers suddenly reveals he or she had the key piece of information and forgot to pass it along in a timely fashion.

This happens in business virtually every day. Someone has a bit of information that may be less than pleasant and delays in delivering it. But, as Sandler's character reminds us, the news isn't going to change. Holding it back only makes the problem worse.

If it happens to you, remind the person who just torpedoed your effort that honesty is always welcome, especially when it is combined with timeliness.

Then feel free to scream: "Another thing you could have told me YESTERDAY!" It won't change anything, but you'll like the moment.

50 First Dates provides a great lesson about paying attention to the customer. The movie pairs Sandler again with Drew Barrymore, his co-star in *The Wedding Singer*. The highly improbable plot has Sandler's character, Henry, falling for Lucy (Barrymore), a young woman with a strange problem. Because of a traffic accident, Lucy has lost her ability to create long-term memories. Every day she wakes up forgetting everything that happened the previous day.

The challenge for Henry is to win the woman he loves despite the fact that every day requires meeting her, attracting her, and building a relationship. As the movie shows us, it's exhausting.

And exhilarating. In one scene, some of Henry's friends comment on how different his relationship is from theirs. Their wives and girlfriends are especially envious that Henry provides so much attention daily when their husbands and boyfriends provide almost none.

The customer parallel is stunning. So often, businesses work incredibly hard at winning the customer for the first time. They woo new customers, flirt, give gifts and all kinds of attention. Then, once the customer is won, businesses drift into the same old/same old. Attention falls off and so does attraction.

As Dr. Laura Berman wrote in her best seller, *Real Women, Real Sex,* the same happens to relationships. At first couples can't get enough of each other and they show their affection by holding hands and exchanging lengthy kisses. In a few years, they air kiss while discussing the kids, the pets and, oh, please take out the garbage.

Berman suggests a daily ten-second kiss to revitalize a relationship. *50 First Dates* suggests never letting the moment get old in much the same way.

Think about the impact it would have on your business if you set out to delight customers every day in the same way you did the first day. They would know you are never taking them for granted, never letting your attention drift to someone or something new. And since the cost of keeping a customer is substantially lower than attracting a new one, the bottom line benefit would be staggering.

Think of the same policy with your associates in your company, too. When we first hire people, we talk about all the wonderful elements of our companies. After a few weeks, the romance is gone, the attention is over, and we simply expect them to do their jobs. When our efforts flag, the same happens to our associates' performance. Let's romance them too, and through our efforts we'll see the benefit to our customers.

Remember, if Adam Sandler could do it, you can, too.

Everybody Needs
a Fish Story

B	BRANDING
	Suggested for all business audiences

JIM DONALD, THE FORMER CEO of both Starbucks and the Pathmark supermarket chain, and now the CEO of the Pacific Northwest grocery chain Haggen, Inc., likes to say that everybody needs to have a "fish story." By that, he means that every person—and every company—needs to have a distinguishing characteristic that makes them top of mind.

I have two. And I figure that they are pretty much responsible for my whole career.

My first fish story is about the three months that I spent in 1977–78 working as a bodyguard for the late Farrah Fawcett.

True story. (I know that you've just gone to the back cover to check me out and see if I resemble anything close to bodyguard material. Sorry to disappoint you. I got the job during the making of her first post-*Charlie's Angels* movie, *Somebody Killed Her Husband*, because I knew the guy running security and he thought it might be worthwhile to have a person who knew something about movies on the team, as opposed to all the oversized ex-football players who made up the rest of her security force.)

Once my stint with Farrah was over, I returned to the task of trying to get a newspaper job. And this is where my second fish story comes in.

In late 1978, Woodward and Bernstein were still folk heroes and everybody wanted to get into journalism, and I had fewer credentials than most. So when I got the opportunity for an interview at the Gannett Westchester Rockland Newspapers, I got my clips together, pulled out my old sports jacket, and set the alarm clock so I wouldn't be late.

I woke up to find that we'd been hit with about two feet of snow. So I dragged my younger brothers out of bed and told them to help dig me out of the driveway. Which they did. And then I made them drive with me to the interview so they could help get me out of any snowdrifts. Which they did. And then, when I got to the newspaper office, I found that the guy who was supposed to interview me hadn't shown up because the blizzard was too much for him.

Still, it was a good move on my part, because I got the reputation within Gannett as being "the guy who showed up." When I got an interview with the then-editor of the *Rockland Journal-News*, I walked into his office and saw Farrah's famous poster on his wall.

I had two fish stories to tell in that interview. Farrah, and the snowstorm. I got the job.

Which brings us to *Tootsie*, one of the funniest movies of all time.

Tootsie tells the story of Michael Dorsey, a New York actor who is obsessed with his art, to the point where he cannot see the big picture. He focuses on finding the truth in every character he plays, even if he's playing a tomato in a television commercial. His obsessions about acting have reached the point where nobody wants to hire him. Not in New York, not in California, not for the stage or for movies or for television.

Through a series of plot twists, Dorsey, played to manic perfection by Dustin Hoffman, who probably shares some of those obsessions, decides to audition for a daytime soap opera. For a woman's role. As a woman. And he gets it. And becomes an enormous hit, even though he is living a lie that makes his life increasingly complicated.

But the real point (spoiler alert here…I have to give away part of the ending) is that when Dorsey finally lets the world know who he is and what he's been doing, he has created for himself a fish story—a story that nobody ever is going to forget. It'll help him get a play about the Love Canal produced, and it'll probably help him get a whole series of parts that he previously would not have been considered for. It may even help him get the girl he loves, played by Jessica Lange, who considered his female alter ego to be her best friend.

In business and in life, we all have to find a differential advantage— the fish story that will get us noticed. That's a message that I give to college students whenever I teach a class, and it is a message that even established businesses and business people need to hear.

Trader Joe's uses the concept of the fish story to great advantage. Virtually every private label item in Trader Joe's, which means almost every item in the store, has a story with it. It makes Trader Joe's different and successful at the same time.

Ben & Jerry's has used its fish story to the hilt, promoting its socially conscious bona fides. Sam Adams beer became the most prominent microbrewery in the country by telling the fish story of how founder Jim Koch found an old family recipe that was better than those used by behemoth brewers. And the fish story is one of the reasons that Newman's Own has thrived, because it has a tale about charitable giving that sets it apart.

So if you don't have a fish story, either for yourself or your business, get one. If that means you have to do something distinctive so you have a story to tell, so be it. That is sort of the point. And if you have one but haven't been telling it, it is time to dust off that narrative and make it work for you.

Nearly Everyone Can Become a Leader

L	LEADERSHIP
	Suggested for all business audiences

THERE IS NO TASK MORE VITAL or more difficult in business than managing and leading others. Sadly, it's easy to argue that there is no task done as poorly. The problem starts with how managers are selected. Think about any company you have worked in and the same pattern is likely to emerge: those who are best at specific tasks are promoted to management.

It's why the "Peter Principle," the maxim that people will rise to their level of incompetence, is so well known. That principle encapsulates the belief that the best at any specific job get promoted until they reach a level of incompetence.

But a contrary point of view comes from Bill North, the former chief executive of Medtronic and the author of *True North*, a book dedicated to helping individuals find the leader inside themselves. North argues that there are no born leaders or, more correctly, that everyone can learn to be a leader.

The movies back him up with lots of fairy tales. Most movies about managers, coaches, and teachers all follow a similar path: well-meaning new leader takes over and fails to connect with the troops. Part of the problem is the manager who over-manages, under-manages, bullies, or tries too hard to be a friend. Part of the problem comes from the team, which turns a deaf ear due to past experience and never gives the new leader a chance.

Suddenly, there is a dramatic event that changes the status quo. The leader seizes a moment to grow and the team opens up. Then great things happen and the movie races to its triumphant conclusion. *Stand and Deliver*, *Remember the Titans*, *To Sir With Love*, and *The Longest Yard* are all examples of movies based on this premise.

Movies of this type convey a feel-good sensation about leadership. But in the movies, managers rarely deal with the challenges that real life presents every day on the job. A lesser-known movie, *Renaissance Man*, offers a more realistic story and one that real life managers can relate to and learn from.

Danny DeVito plays Bill Rago, a Detroit-based advertising executive who loses his job at the start of the movie. Set in 1994, Detroit is a tough place to find employment, so Bill accepts a position teaching remedial English to Army enlistees. He arrives with an attitude of cynicism and apathy that is obvious immediately to his class and a drill sergeant played by Gregory Hines.

The students understand they need education to help them succeed in the military and respond by pushing Bill to teach them. One day, while doing a reading assignment, the students turn the tables on Bill to find out what he's reading. It turns out to be Shakespeare's *Hamlet*. Bill describes the murder, intrigue, plotting, and intricacies, and the class is enthralled.

But like too many managers, Bill still isn't responding to his team. His efforts are half-hearted and both success and connection elude him. Finally, he shows up late for class and finds his students gone. For the first time, Bill decides to fight back. He tracks the group to the enormous climbing tower that dominates the base. The students are stunned to see Bill climb the tower, but are even more surprised when he undertakes the harder task—rappelling down the side. He descends the tower horribly, but once on the ground, his commitment to the students is clear.

With that act, he finally becomes the leader the class seeks. Together they start to progress until Bill sees the fruits of his labors in two ways. First, he hears a student answer a challenge from the drill sergeant by reciting the famed St. Crispin's Day speech from *Henry V* ("We few, we happy few, we band of brothers..."). The moment stuns the drill sergeant as he realizes that the English classes are helping his charges develop the pride and commitment he seeks in soldiers.

A second moment comes when one student rejects portraying a specific character in *Hamlet* whom he think is a loser. As he provides a vivid argument in support of his decision, he demonstrates how much of the complex story he has absorbed. By the time we reach the conclusion, the students have grown, and so has their teacher. His cynicism and apathy have been replaced by commitment and engagement.

Most managers toil in quiet, making companies run efficiently and effectively in countless ways. Chief executives recognize the importance of good managers and their ability to get the highest level of performance from their team. Legendary stories about managers come from Procter & Gamble, where CEOs long asked for information about people, not products. Another comes from independent retailer Norman Mayne, who once said that his employees were more important than shoppers, because they controlled the fate of his family's three Dorothy Lane supermarkets.

We all can remember managers who made our lives terrible through uneven rules, favoritism, vague directions, and micromanaging. We can also recall managers who made a difference, by daring us and helping us to improve, knowing that our success would reflect well on them.

It's impossible to write this chapter without examining the flaws of the manager I know best: me. Many years ago, I found myself promoted to a position of authority at a fairly young age due to a series of strange circumstances. Immediately, I set about to mess up the opportunity as I worked diligently at staying friends with my co-workers instead of providing leadership.

Luckily, my company did me a great favor. A personnel consultant was brought in to run an evaluation of select managers, including me. Of course, I expected a glowing report, but I got a wake-up call instead. Years later, I can still remember the comment that got to me. One person on my staff wrote something like, "Michael needs to lead; if he takes this seriously, so will we."

I was like Bill in *Renaissance Man*. I wasn't giving the job my all, and my team struggled because of my failures. My fondest hope today is that the same person would not make that comment again. Of course, even if they didn't, I'm sure there are many other faults they'd find.

And hopefully, like Bill Rago, I'd find the willingness to learn and grow.

Go the Opposite Way

RB	RULE BREAKERS
P	PLANNING
Suggested for all business audiences	

SO, YOU THINK YOU'VE HAD A BAD DAY. Believe me, it could be far worse.

Consider a scene from the Mel Brooks comedy *Young Frankenstein.* In the scene, Gene Wilder's character, Fredrick Frankenstein, is in a graveyard digging up a body with his faithful assistant Igor, played by Marty Feldman.

The well-known Frankenstein story of the re-animation of a dead body has been made countless times, but never like *Young Frankenstein,* where horror gives way to a heavy dose of slapstick.

The graveyard scene speaks to us all. Knee deep in a cold grave, Frankenstein says, "What a filthy job," to which Igor responds, "It could be worse." In disbelief, Frankenstein asks "How?"

Igor says, "It could be raining." A split-second later, we hear a crack of thunder and, of course, rain comes pouring down.

Be honest, you've had days like that.

In the midst of the movie's mayhem, we find a wonderful little business example.

When we first meet Frankenstein (pronounced "Fronk-en-steen" in this movie), he is a serious doctor teaching medical school. He dismisses his grandfather as a cuckoo and his work as "doo-doo." But he travels to Transylvania and discovers his grandfather's secret lab and the book that details how the elder Frankenstein made his monster come to life. As Dr. Frankenstein reads, he suddenly realizes the genius in his grandfather's plans.

"Until from the midst of this darkness, a sudden light broke in upon me. A light so brilliant and wondrous and yet so simple. Change the poles from plus to minus and from minus to plus," he reads. He then realizes that his grandfather's experiment could actually work.

He sets about to re-animate his own monster. Only in *Young Frankenstein,* instead of killing the villagers, the monster sings, dances, and makes love with amazing results. Plus he ends up on Wall Street, which might help explain a lot of the activity in the financial community over the past few years.

But, for our business lesson, we need to focus on Wilder's discovery. A plan he had completely dismissed suddenly makes sense when looking at it from a different angle.

Think of how many times we experience that. We have a problem and we work it again and again, the exact same way each time. Then someone else sees it and suggests a simple change and it's genius.

There are many examples of this process in the business world. Herb Kelleher, Southwest Airline's founder, talked about all the conventions he shattered on the way to success, including using lesser-known airports to cut costs and flying only one kind of plane to create efficiencies in repairs and parts.

Reversing the pluses and minuses can lead to profound change. Today, few of us know Shai Agassi, but that may soon change. Agassi is working on a radical proposal for electric cars that completely shifts the way people drive and get fuel. Agassi's idea is to make car purchases like cell phone purchases: a small amount paid for the vehicle and charges shifted based on use. Community electrical charging stations would be built to allow people to use electric cars in ways that fit their lifestyles.

Is it, as Dr. Frankenstein would say, "cuckoo?" Or is it someone who just looked at an old problem and switched the plus and minus to solve it? Only time will tell.

In the meantime, *Young Frankenstein* reminds us to laugh, to remember that things can and will get worse, and that sometimes the only way to solve a problem is by turning it on its head.

Make the Right Decisions

E	ETHICS
L	LEADERSHIP
Suggested for all business audiences	

DEFENDING YOUR LIFE ISN'T JUST THE INCOMPARABLE Albert Brooks's best movie, it probably would make a top-20 list of my favorite movies of all time. Not just because it is very funny, not just because it has an innovative premise to which it adheres faithfully, but because it is the best kind of comedy—truthful.

The movie starts out with Daniel Miller (played by Brooks, who also wrote and directed the movie) celebrating his birthday. Miller accidentally crashes his brand new BMW into a city bus and dies. He finds himself in Judgment City, which has everything from office complexes to hotels to comedy clubs to golf courses. Judgment City serves as a way station for souls while it is being determined by a trial whether they can move on to the next phase of existence. Miller is represented by Bob Diamond (Rip Torn) and the prosecution represented by Lena Foster (Lee Grant).

It isn't an easy trial, because Miller has lived a life of compromise and fear, never asserting himself or giving of himself while on Earth.

He's frustrated by his own mediocrity, which is shown to him in the courtroom via videos of specific days in his own life. He defends his life, but it rings hollow. Miller knows he has not lived up to his own potential.

However, if miracles can happen, why not in Judgment City? Miller meets Julia, played by a luminous Meryl Streep, who has lived a good and virtuous and compassionate life. In short, she is everything that Daniel is not. They fall in love but are destined to be separated, since she is moving on to the next phase of existence and he most certainly is not. Daniel doesn't make things any better when he declines to sleep with Julia, and the judges determine that he is simply afraid.

Now, this is a romantic comedy and a Hollywood movie, so there's a happy ending. It actually is through his love for Julia that Daniel overcomes his fears and is judged ready for the next step in the universal food chain. But there is a serious lesson in this movie, one that applies to both personal conduct and business. We should make decisions that are the right thing to do.

We all can think of times when we made decisions that probably wouldn't be defensible when called on the carpet in Judgment City. I like to call these "*Defending Your Life* moments." But there is no example of a decision more startling than that of Peanut Corporation of America (PCA), which sent out peanut butter tainted with salmonella that sickened more than 600 people and caused perhaps as many as nine deaths in 2009. There were more than 2,200 products recalled as a result of the contamination. According to the *Washington Post*, federal investigators said that they believed that PCA's president, Stewart Parnell, knew about the contamination but didn't do anything about the cause, including a hole in the roof that allowed bird feces to fall on the manufacturing equipment, because he was concerned about the costs.

Parnell and other company executives actually had their own "*Defending Your Life* moments" when they appeared before Congress and were asked if they'd be willing to eat any products made with peanut butter from their plant. They declined.

There is no Hollywood happy ending for this story. PCA only made one percent of the country's peanut butter, but the crisis affected almost everyone as shoppers simply stopped buying the product. PCA only made peanut butter that was sold to companies for use in other formulations such as ice cream or birdseed, but even brands like Skippy and Peter Pan suffered because shopper confidence was eroded. And I would argue that this was just one of a continuing series of food safety missteps that have affected everything from spinach to tomatoes to pistachios. PCA managed to hurt everyone in the food business.

All because of greed. All because they knew the right thing to do, but didn't do it.

Good lesson here for business. Decisions have consequences. In this life, and in the hereafter.

Take a New Perspective

E	ETHICS
RB	**RULE BREAKERS**
P	**PLANNING**
Suggested for all business audiences	

WHEN FACING A CHALLENGING PROBLEM, sometimes the best way to proceed is to invent a new solution, rather than relying on a tried and true answer that might not fit the new dynamics.

The business world is packed with companies that caught lightning in a bottle and revolutionized businesses by solving an old problem with a completely new idea. Whether it's FedEx revolutionizing overnight shipping or Enterprise building a car rental giant by focusing on auto repair shops instead of airports, it happens again and again.

The film *Working Girl* demonstrates an innovative solution to a business problem. This movie was a celebration of the go-go period on Wall Street, with a very different take than the dark *Wall Street* that came out a year earlier. In that powerful drama, a young stockbroker discovers the corrosive power of greed and unbridled ambition in the world of high finance. In *Working Girl*, a young secretary learns how to get ahead, but also how difficult the game gets when you start playing at a new level.

The heroine, Tess McGill, played by Melanie Griffith, wants a brighter future, but the world conspires to hold her down. Her bosses ignore her and her friends urge her to seek a more modest life. But Tess won't give up. She concocts a creative merger plan that her boss, Katharine Parker, played by Sigourney Weaver, laughs off, and then secretly steals to engineer it without Tess. When Parker is injured skiing, Tess uncovers the plot and launches her own response, helping put the merger together herself.

In the process, Tess pulls off moves only achievable in film. She unwittingly drafts as a partner Parker's boyfriend, Jack Trainer (Harrison Ford), winning him as both a business partner and lover in the process. Against all odds, the team brings the merger to conclusion.

Hollywood happy endings reign supreme as Tess not only produces a business success, but also humiliates her deceptive boss in the process. Since life is rarely like a movie, there's little to learn in that. But there is much to learn in how she builds the deal.

Tess puts together an unlikely merger after she sees two unrelated items in a daily newspaper. One item involves a charity event being run by the daughter of a company's CEO and a radio shock jock; the second is a business article about how the same company was looking to expand to media. The items gave her the flash of inspiration to build an unexpected deal merging the two companies.

Working Girl gives us two lessons that are too easily forgotten by business these days. First, that idealism can matter. Tess is a rare character in a movie set in the mergers and acquisitions climate of late 1980s Wall Street. Rather than working for fortune or power, Tess is trying to make a beneficial deal and prove herself in an unkind world. Her character could be seen as naïve, but we root for her honesty and drive.

But the second lesson has much greater real world value. Tess finds the creative and unexpected solution by simply keeping her eyes open. It's a valuable trait that is useful in real life as well as in movies.

In the early part of the 20th century, a young mother had a problem.

Cooking and straining vegetables for her infant was an incredible time commitment. One day she asked her husband why the canning company he ran couldn't help her with this problem. His name was Daniel Frank Gerber, and the problem his wife found at home launched a successful baby food company and an entirely new business.

Many years later, Charles "Mike" Harper had a mild heart attack while on a business trip. After he recovered, Harper set out to eat a healthier diet, but found the choices facing him were unappetizing or too time consuming. Luckily, Harper was the CEO of ConAgra foods and thanks to his medical awakening, Healthy Choice products were born. In a similar burst of insight, the Sony Walkman, the pioneer in personal listening devices, was created out of a request from the company chairman who wanted to listen to opera recordings on his frequent transpacific trips.

Brainstorms happen in many ways. A few years back, I saw one occur. While recruiting speakers for an executive conference, I scheduled Regina Herzlinger, a Harvard professor with some radical views on reforming health care.

On the day of the speech, Herzlinger was unable to appear because of a massive snowstorm. Rather than simply drop this important topic, we had her speak by phone to the crowd of nearly 750, not knowing if the message would succeed. Our answer came quickly at the end of the speech when the CEO of Safeway Stores, Steve Burd, took to the podium to echo Herlzinger's comments. Within months, Burd began spearheading a massive corporate effort to overhaul thinking on health care.

Given the ferocity of the health care debate in the U.S., Burd was taking a significant risk. But he soon began speaking widely on the topics of linking health care to better and healthier lifestyles and improved consumer behavior in shopping for medical assistance. Burd, whose positions can be found on the Safeway website, took his new approach to his company, to labor unions with whom he previously had an extremely difficult relationship, and government leaders.

And it all began with a single speech. As *Working Girl* shows us, sometimes new ideas come from unexpected places. If you are not trapped into giving a predictable response, you may come up with an innovative solution to a new business problem.

Anyone Can Be a Hero

RB	RULE BREAKERS
L	LEADERSHIP
Suggested for all business audiences	

THE SUBJECTS OF BIOGRAPHICAL FILMS usually need little introduction. In almost all cases, they are household names or people whose deeds speak volumes about their character, drive, and ability to rise above great handicaps.

Charlie Wilson was not a household name, but his accomplishments are worthy of a motion picture. Wilson, a member of the U.S. House of Representatives for 24 years, loved liquor, fast and beautiful women, and being part of the system. In short, Wilson was a pretty typical congressman, and not exactly hero material.

Charlie Wilson's War, a wonderfully entertaining picture, depicts this congressman as flawed, yet able to play a pivotal role during a singular moment in history. In doing so, the movie provides the first of two great lessons: heroes can come from every walk of life and frequently don't wear halos. Sometimes they are just looking for a party, but wind up doing something extraordinary.

The film follows Wilson literally from a hot tub party to a ceremony celebrating his role in the fall of the Soviet Union. It is a fun and insightful story, wonderfully acted by Tom Hanks, Julia Roberts, Phillip Seymour Hoffman, and Amy Adams.

As the movie opens in 1980, Wilson is in Las Vegas, surrounded in the hot tub by naked women. He is struggling to listen to a report on *60 Minutes* by Dan Rather, who was undercover with freedom fighters in Afghanistan, reporting on the appalling lack of weaponry and support they had to resist the invasion of the Soviet Union. The Cold War raged very hot.

Wilson decides something must be done. With seemingly little thought, he manages to double the budget of the covert operations supporting Afghanistan. His action draws praise from two very different people: Joanne Herring, a wealthy Texas socialite dedicated to fighting communism, played by Roberts, and a coarse CIA agent played by Hoffman. Hoffman is a loose but brilliant cannon, with a plan for a U.S. role in Afghanistan. When they first meet, Hanks tells Hoffman, "You are no James Bond," to which Hoffman responds, "Well you ain't Thomas Jefferson."

While the socialite pushes Wilson for more action, the CIA agent starts directing Wilson toward the right weapons, the right allies, and the right strategy to win. Slowly but surely, Wilson influences Congress, gains access to increasing supplies of money, and gets cooperation from both the Israelis and Egyptians. He manages to do all of this while avoiding indictment on a drug investigation being handled by a U.S. Attorney named Rudy Giuliani.

Sometimes history is way more fun than fiction.

Surprisingly, the clandestine strategy in Afghanistan starts working. In fact, some of the scenes showing refugee camps and the Soviet air campaign in Afghanistan are the most stunning of the film. At first we see the Soviet army shooting up villages, animals, and people at will. We see the teeming mass of humanity in Pakistan and hear about the bombs, the shootings, and the land mines left to maim and injure children. Then, suddenly, we see a change as the rebels—the Mujahedeen—master their surface-to-air missiles and begin fighting back. The tide turns, and the Soviets start to lose the war.

119

We watch Wilson's war grow in scope and cost, as more members of Congress comprehend the stakes and the opportunity. As we know from history, the Soviets finally were so bloodied and wearied by Afghanistan that they pulled out, and the wounds were deep. In short order the might of the "Evil Empire" began to crumble, and within a few short years after the withdrawal from Afghanistan, the USSR was gone.

Charlie Wilson, the least likely of heroes, played an enormous role.

The clear message is that anyone can play a significant role in great causes by thinking big and taking action where none was expected. It reminds us that even the most insignificant among us (and Wilson was one of the lesser-regarded members of Congress) can make great things happen.

But the movie takes pains to make a major second point: finish the job.

Late in the movie, while Wilson and others celebrate the victory and the stunning change in global fortunes, Hoffman's CIA agent delivers one last message. Afghanistan, he reminds Wilson, is a mess after nine years of war. He urges Wilson to find a way to finish the job by helping to rebuild the war-torn country so that a new generation can grow up there with hope. Sadly, Wilson loses this battle in Congress.

History shows what happened with this failed opportunity. Within a few years, Afghanistan fell into chaos, allowing the Taliban to take over the country with a radical form of Islam never before seen on earth. The Taliban in turn gave sanctuary to a training center for the terror group Al Qaeda and its leader, Osama bin Laden. And in September 2001, the entire U.S. became very aware of the fruits of the job left unfinished in Afghanistan.

The closing screen credits of *Charlie Wilson's War* makes the connection painfully clear for the viewer. It recounts how history was changed before "we f****d up the end game."

So yes, a less than heroic type can be a hero. Yes, a single person can make history by channeling energy and efforts properly. And yes, a single person can make a difference.

But all of that won't matter if you don't see the job all the way through.

Don't Run Your Life and Business by the Numbers

RB	RULE BREAKERS
E	ETHICS
Suggested for all business audiences	

FROM THE OPENING MOMENTS OF *Stranger than Fiction*, the audience is put on notice that this movie isn't going to be by the numbers.

We hear a woman's voice talking about a man named Harold Crick, played by Will Ferrell. She is describing his actions as we see them onscreen:

"Harold Crick was a man of infinite numbers, endless calculations, and remarkably few words…Every weekday, for twelve years, Harold would brush each of his thirty-two teeth seventy-six times. Thirty-eight times back and forth, thirty-eight times up and down. Every weekday, for twelve years, Harold would tie his tie in a single Windsor knot instead of the double, thereby saving up to forty-three seconds."

Harold Crick, you see, is the ultimate numbers guy. He is a senior auditor for the Internal Revenue Service, a man living both alone and insulated, without humor or irony or even ambition, satisfied with a by-the-numbers existence in which he never steps on the cracks on the sidewalk, counts every step he takes, and knows precisely how many open seats there are on the bus he's on.

In a sense, Harold is like so many people in so many businesses, totally addicted to the numbers and unable to see the big picture, unable to perceive or take pleasure in the world around him.

He is thrown off his game by a voice, a distinctive woman's voice, that seems to be describing his life, not just the mundane details, but also his feelings and perceptions. The voice belongs to author Karen Eiffel (Emma Thompson). Harold is in a *Twilight Zone*-type situation. He is a character not just in his own life, but also in her unfinished novel, and they seem to be unfolding simultaneously, with one very specific problem. Karen has referred obliquely to Harold's upcoming death, which has sent him into a panic trying to figure out: one, why his life is being narrated, and two, how he can avoid dying.

This strange confluence of events shakes Harold's sense of complacency down to its core. He finds himself inexplicably attracted to Ana (Maggie Gyllenhaal), a baker he is auditing. She's a woman with an extravagant tattoo and a little bit of the anarchist in her; a woman with whom, under usual circumstances, he would never be fascinated. Suddenly his inhibitions begin to break down and the world becomes a little more colorful. Harold begins to embrace the fact he may be about die, and he begins to actually live his life. All of it. He learns to play the guitar, stops wearing a tie, even brushes his teeth differently. These actions open his heart and mind and spirit, and allow for the possibility not only that he could love the baker, but that she could love him.

This is a wonderful lesson for any business. We all know companies where so much time is spent paying attention to the spreadsheets and quarterly numbers that they squeeze all the life and creativity out of the business. Think of the senior executives who have been brought on board simply to cut costs, slash personnel, and pay attention to margins and stock quotes. While that might be a good strategy in the short term, it almost never makes sense in the long term. Most businesses cannot thrive without empowering innovative and creative people to not just *do* their best, but to *be* their best.

There is a wonderfully evocative moment in the film when Ana offers Harold a cookie, fresh and soft and warm from the oven. "I don't like cookies," Harold says. She looks at him disbelievingly. Everybody likes cookies, she says. Not Harold, who was raised in a family where his mother didn't bake and only served packaged cookies. Ana gives him a warm chocolate chip cookie, and commands him to dip it in a glass of cold milk and eat it. Which he does. And it is one of the most sensuous experiences of his life. From that moment on, he'll never be the same.

Stranger than Fiction is a terrific movie. Ferrell, Gyllenhaal, and Thompson have never been better or more nuanced, and both Dustin Hoffman and Queen Latifah deliver excellent supporting turns. The direction by Marc Forster and the writing by Zach Helm are utterly delightful. But beyond the move's cinematic pleasures, *Stranger than Fiction* offers a metaphor for business and for life.

Watch it. Share it. Enjoy it. And while you're at it, have a cookie. Preferably fresh-baked.

You Can Succeed Without a Gold Medal

RB	RULE BREAKERS
L	LEADERSHIP
Suggested for all business audiences	

IF THE BASIC STORY OF *Cool Runnings* weren't true, filmgoers would have rejected the movie as too much fantasy to bother watching. It's a funny film layered on top of a true story that provides business lessons in perseverance, creativity, problem solving, and self worth, with special emphasis on the last.

The story begins with our hero, Derice Bannock (Leon Robinson), training for the Olympic trials in Jamaica. Bannock, a top sprinter, is hoping to represent his country and win the gold medal, much as his father did decades before. Jamaica produces top sprinters, and Bannock is considered a likely champion.

But fate intervenes when the runner next to Bannock falls and pulls Bannock and a second runner down with him. We see the agony etched in Bannock's face as he watches the winners celebrate at the end of the track, and we sympathize with him while he pleads in vain for a re-running of the race.

Bannock isn't beaten for long. While losing his argument at the office of the head of the Olympic committee, he sees a picture of his father with an unknown man. The second man, he is told, is a former bobsled champion who came to Jamaica with a idea to use the island's speedy runners to revolutionize the winter sport. Denied his path to the Olympics, Bannock immediately hatches a plan, though he admits he knows nothing about the bobsled.

With his best friend, Sanka Coffie (that's his name and more strange ones follow), at his side, he searches out the bobsled champion now living in Jamaica. And Bannock quickly discovers that the champion, Irv Blitzer, played by John Candy just before his death, is big, angry, and has no interest in bobsledding anymore. Bannock, however, won't relent and finally Blitzer agrees to talk with him.

The plot comically follows the crew struggling to assemble a team, scraping up the money for the trip to the winter Olympics, and learning, against all odds, how to bobsled and deal with cold weather, two challenges they were poorly prepared to face. Along the way, we learn the reasons each of the teammates has for participating in the enterprise: strong man Yul Brenner (yes, another name in the movie) who is dying to get out of Jamaica; Junior Bevil, who wants to chart a path free of his father; and Blitzer, who is looking for redemption in the world of bobsledding that he left in shame after being caught cheating.

Throughout the movie, they encounter a combination of racism and disbelief in their skills that causes nearly every part of the bobsled establishment to throw hurdles in their path. But we also watch them work increasingly hard to surmount the challenges.

The transformation complete, the team becomes a competitive force and their tiny island nation rallies behind them.

One of the more interesting aspects of the story is the lack of a fairy tale ending. While the Jamaicans improve and gain respect on the slopes, they end their Olympic dream in a terrible crash on the track, wrecking their sled, which is named "Cool Runnings." In the process, however, they realize all they have accomplished by giving their best effort. It's a refreshing story in a time when "win at all costs" is frequently a philosophy of competition.

The personal growth stories contain the best business lessons, and no lesson is better than Blitzer's. Throughout the film we see his struggles. A one-time Olympic champion, he is now a subject of ridicule because of his cheating. Late in the movie, Bannock finally confronts Blitzer about why he cheated.

Blitzer admits that he simply couldn't picture his life without winning. But he has learned a lesson from his past: "A gold medal is a wonderful thing. But if you're not enough without one, you'll never be enough with one."

It's a lesson everyone in business (and life) should remember. If we aren't enough *without* the corner office, the fancy car, the large home, the nice clothes, or whatever else it may be, we aren't enough *with* them, either. Blitzer's redemption was not winning; it was making an honest effort against the odds.

Many of us need to think the same way. Are we proud of our efforts or just the recognition we receive? Are we satisfied when we look in the mirror each morning? Are we proud of the person we are?

It's not a small question nor is it one easily or lightly asked. And for all the fun and laughs of *Cool Runnings*, the movie takes the question and the answer seriously. Just as we all should.

Don't be Foolishly Consistent

RB	RULE BREAKERS
Suggested for all business audiences	

NOTED PSYCHOLOGIST ABRAHAM MASLOW once commented, "If the only tool you have is a hammer, you will see every problem as a nail."

Since only a small percentage of problems are "nails," sometimes we have to face the fact that we need a different tool. Luckily, most of us can adjust to a change of circumstances.

But not everyone can, and few can do it all the time. Some people in the workplace maintain a stubborn devotion to a plan, a solution, or a theory that defies all rational thinking. These misguided workers persist in approaching a problem the same way, no matter how the situation is changing around them. While dedication and fortitude can be admirable, we think an old saying is an apt lesson here: a foolish consistency is the hobgoblin of small minds.

Luckily, there is a movie that makes this very point, but unluckily, it isn't a great movie. But in this case the lack of quality is completely acceptable. After all, the punishment for stubbornness needs (to paraphrase the very funny *Animal House)* an example so low and stupid

127

that it matches the situation. For these moments I give you *Talladega Nights,* a parody of stock car racing with Will Ferrell that ranges from laugh-inducing to eye-rolling.

The movie tells us the story of Ricky Bobby, a caricature of the worst of the racecar set. Bobby, we learn, was born to racing after he was delivered in his father's hot rod moving at who-knows-what speed. Ricky's story gets only more bizarre from there.

The plot defies a quick summary, but it really doesn't matter in this light farce. It's sufficient to say that Bobby becomes a reckless champion of a racer who has a stunning fall from grace. At his low point he is delivering pizzas by bicycle because of his inability to drive, is living with his mother and two monster children, and has given up any hopes of being a racecar driver. Of course, he finds his way back to love, family, and success.

Along the way, we are treated to Ferrell running around a race track in his briefs as he claims, incorrectly, that he is on fire; his wife asking the doctor to pull the plug on him in the hospital while he is fully awake; his wife and best friend deciding to marry a few short days later and asking him to attend the wedding; and more mayhem, thanks to Sacha Baron Cohen, John C. Reilly, Amy Adams, and others. Molly Shannon is fabulous as the constantly inebriated wife of the owner of Bobby's car.

The story may be thin, but the lesson for the stubborn among us is very simple. Bobby's life on the racetrack has been shaped by a single phrase uttered by his frequently drunk and occasionally stoned father, Reece, during a "bring your Dad to school" day. The elder Bobby tells the class that his philosophy is "if you aren't first, you're last." The phrase is idiotic, but the younger Bobby takes it to heart.

Once he becomes a racecar driver we see how the philosophy shapes him. Bobby is a reckless driver doing everything and anything to win a race. He causes accidents, ignores his friends, and takes from, but never helps, his fellow drivers, all in pursuit of his simple mantra: "If you aren't first, you're last."

Late in the movie, when Bobby's father has helped his son regain his confidence about driving, the son utters the famous phrase. His father tells him that it is the stupidest thing he has ever heard, reminding Ricky that there is second, third, fourth…loads of places other than first and last.

Honestly, it's not a great scene. But as a lesson in how *not* to do things, it is pretty good.

Bobby, after all, is a caricature. He's a fool and a one-dimensional character, created for laughter. In the workplace, the stubborn among us are rarely that harmless.

Instead, we run into countless people who face situations with the same simple-mindedness of Bobby's mantra. We read about generals who are fighting the last war, which is why the new wars start so poorly. Likewise, economists fight the last recession, which produces similarly weak results. And countless businesses have gotten into trouble by stubbornly sticking to the strategy that served them in the past, even when the variables have changed.

Real life is complex. Businesses have to lean on and return to their strengths to get through tough times. Going back to the basics that made a company or individual great is frequently the best path to solve any problem.

But we also have to recognize when the situation has been altered. We have to recognize how new competitors, new consumer needs, new technological challenges, or even new world conditions can upset the status quo and force us to change tactics. The change could be the Prius, Whole Foods, high speed Internet, rising gas prices, declining gas prices, terrorism…well, you name it. The common denominator is that all these factors and many more can change the game. Those who don't change strategy quickly will pay with permanent irrelevance.

Sure, *Talladega Nights* isn't one of history's great movies. It might not even rate as a good movie. But it's worth watching so you can laugh at Ricky Bobby and then ask yourself: am I any better?

Remember that the maxim, "if you aren't first, you're last," is true only when there are only two in the race.

"Take Five"

DATE MOVIES

Cross The Thin Line Between Good and Great

L	LEADERSHIP
	Suggested for all business audiences

WERE IT NOT FOR *The Godfather*, *Bull Durham* might be considered the greatest movie for business lessons of all time. Sure, it's a light-hearted sports film/buddy movie/romantic comedy. But it is so much more.

Bull Durham shows us the great power of sports metaphors. They allow us to witness greatness and weakness, success and failure in ways that both infuriate us and inspire us, but rarely ever hurt us. (Unless you happen to be a Chicago Cubs fan, of course). *Bull Durham* does all of this while making us think, laugh, and feel for the characters in ways that are genuine.

The story is simple: an older player is sent to tutor a younger, high-potential performer in the ways of the game. He succeeds, although in doing so, he recognizes the end of his own career in baseball.

The older player teaches his protégé the importance of teamwork, of focus, and of discipline. He teaches him the realities of growing up and understanding the business in which he toils. He teaches him skills on and off the field. And he teaches him how to be a winner and how to learn from success and failure.

But honestly, it is much more fun than that.

Throw in a highly colorful pack of teammates whose immaturity and various beliefs (yes, voodoo and baseball come together in this film) make for endlessly zany moments.

Throw in a manager who, when frustrated with his team, stages one of the best tantrums you will ever see.

Throw in the tinny sights and sounds of minor league baseball played in ramshackle stadiums with crazy crowd stunts, clueless announcers, and long bus rides.

And throw in that both men compete for the affections of the same woman, who manages to turn baseball, Edith Piaf, and Walt Whitman poetry into sexually charged events. If you have never seen *Bull Durham*, be warned: it earns its R rating with language, piles of sexual innuendo, and more, unless you rent the sanitized television version. The love interest, Annie Savoy, played by Susan Sarandon, adds lessons on focus, discipline, and relaxation, all delivered in an incredibly sensual manner.

With all that, one lesson stands head and shoulders above the rest: the tiny difference between being good and being great.

The lesson is delivered towards the end of the movie when the younger player, Ebbie Calvin "Nuke" LaLoosh (Tim Robbins), receives word of his promotion to the major leagues. Gleeful beyond description, LaLoosh is stunned to find a less than supportive reception from his mentor, "Crash" Davis (Kevin Costner). Davis, who is drunk and more than a little bitter, lays out the difference between good and great in baseball terms:

"You know what the difference is between hitting .250 and hitting .300? I got it figured out. Twenty-five hits a year in 500 at bats is 50 points. Okay. There's six months in a season, that's about 25 weeks. You get one extra flare a week—just one—a gork, a ground ball with eyes, a dying quail—just one more dying quail a week and you're in Yankee Stadium."

In short, just one extra good break, lucky or from hard work, is the difference between a career in the minors and one at the top level.

It's that way in business, too. The difference between good and great is the subject of countless books. But in truth, it's very simple: one better interaction with a customer, one better hiring decision, one bit of extra effort on design, marketing, manufacturing, efficiency, logistics...you name it. One bit of that week after week and your company is humming.

Conversely, the lack of that one break and your company and your career might struggle. And just like in baseball, you have to manufacture that break week after week or you fall off the pedestal.

Sure, talent matters, but talent isn't enough. LaLoosh, as we can see from the very first sports segment of the film, is swimming in talent, but he doesn't know how to channel it. Davis is talented, too, but at a completely different level. And despite his mental focus and intelligence, he only reaches the major leagues for a paltry 21 days in his entire career.

Success, as *Bull Durham* reminds us, never comes easily. It's a prize that requires talent and dedication; persistence and luck. But the message is clear as day that the difference between good and great is very, very small. And must be seized daily.

KEVIN'S POV:

There is a wonderful line in *Bull Durham* when Crash Davis says that baseball must be played "with fear and arrogance." That's a great metaphor for how to conduct oneself in business. You have to be arrogant enough to believe that your product, whatever it happens to be, achieves a level of differentiated excellence that will compel people to buy it. But you also have to be a little bit fearful of failure. Intel's Andrew S. Grove put it best when he said, "only the paranoid survive."

Paranoia—fear of failure—can keep you sharp, can keep you

innovating. You can't be trapped or paralyzed by your fear (that's where the arrogance has to kick in), but it's good to proceed from the premise that if you don't work harder and smarter than everybody else, you're not going to be successful.

Fear and arrogance. Prime ingredients for business success.

Use Word-of-Mouth Advertising

CF	CUSTOMER FOCUS
	Suggested for all business audiences

IN THE COUNTLESS FILMS MADE THROUGH THE YEARS, there are arguably only a handful of scenes so powerful and so memorable that even the casual viewer would see them as spectacular. One of the best comes from the light romantic comedy *When Harry Met Sally*. It also provides an example of one of the most important tenets of business: a happy customer sells the product.

The movie tracks the relationship of Harry and Sally from college through to their early 30s and through countless meanderings in their lives and their mutual relationship. At their first meeting, neither one likes the other very much. Harry, played by Billy Crystal, argues that men and women cannot be friends if they have any attraction to each other. Sally, played by Meg Ryan, says the opposite is true.

Both are proven right. Reunited a few years later, Harry and Sally are both in crisis. Harry is wounded by his sudden divorce. Sally is grappling with the collapse of her long-term relationship. In this prototypical romantic comedy, we follow the two as they build a wonderful friendship and finally realize the love they are seeking lies with the other.

It's a joyous little ride that is easy and fun to watch. But it also provides a showstopper of a scene.

In a critical moment, Harry is bragging to Sally about his prowess as a lover. When Sally asks him how he knows he is so good, Harry assures her he can tell because the women he sleeps with always are satisfied. She points out that they could be faking it, but he says he's absolutely sure that this never has been the case. Sally then provides a bit of acting you will not forget.

Sitting across the table from Harry in a crowded New York City restaurant, Sally suddenly descends into rapture. She moans and groans; she tosses her hair and starts moving spasmodically. Harry is stunned, but Sally won't stop. She continues her acting, concluding what can only be described as a shattering sexual climax all while sitting alone on a seat in the restaurant. She finishes, smiles, and takes another bite of her lunch.

Then comes the kicker that makes the scene so memorable. A woman seated one booth over, having watched the entire display, turns to the waiter and says, "I'll have what she's having." Absolutely hilarious!

And a great business lesson, too. We all know the power of the satisfied consumer, even though most customers do not reach the enjoyment level that Sally has just demonstrated. The satisfied shopper smiles, looks happy, and passes her message of contentment on to everyone around her. In contrast, the dissatisfied shopper also passes his or her mood on. In addition, the dissatisfied shopper is more likely than a satisfied shopper to talk about what happened and spread the word of the poor experience to others.

The examples of how to create a "Sally" moment are all around us. Visitors to Disney properties get it all the time, leaving the theme parks singing and smiling (except for the exhausted children) and telling everyone about the cleanliness, the helpful employees and more. Costco shoppers talk about the sampling stations; Publix customers talk about the kindness of employees; at Nordstrom, people love the extreme level of attention. Even shoppers at CarMax regale you with tales of the joys of buying a used car in a transparent and fair environment.

In short, the great experience is shared and like the woman sitting next to Sally, we all say, "I'll have what she's having."

But it doesn't happen easily. The businesses that deliver this kind of experience must emphasize the need for excellence to all their employees. Everyone has to be on his or her game to make it happen. And unlike Harry, we can't assume that our performance is always outstanding. Instead, we need to talk to our shoppers to determine if we are really delivering.

Sadly, poor customer service happens with far greater frequency than world-class service. Two years ago, I found myself crammed into the middle seat on a United Airlines flight from Denver to Washington, D.C., and I had no chance to eat before the flight. I bought one of United's "snacks" and discovered to my horror that one of the packaged items had long since passed its "use by" date.

I have worked with the food industry for a number of years, and I believe in treating "use by" dates seriously. I pointed out the problem to the flight attendant. Unfortunately, her response was to assure me the product was safe, which I explained was a ridiculous claim. At that moment, no one sitting near me was thinking, "I'll have what he's having." In fact, I could hear everyone checking the dates on their packages as person after person hit their call buttons to return the item right after me.

That is the most important lesson we get from Sally's demonstration. Making sure that customers are truly satisfied is not easy, but there is little in business that is more important.

KEVIN'S POV:

A quick note here. The woman who delivered the "I'll have what she's having" line is, in fact, director Rob Reiner's mother, Estelle Reiner.

Which proves yet another important life/business maxim: Mom knows best.

Don't Be a One-Hit Wonder

B	BRANDING
CF	CUSTOMER FOCUS
P	PLANNING

Suggested for all business audiences

"THERE ARE NO SECOND ACTS IN AMERICAN LIVES," wrote F. Scott Fitzgerald. It is very hard to duplicate success, and often difficult to live up to the great expectations that come with accomplishment.

And sometimes the audience isn't ready for the second act, especially if it's not what it was expecting. There's a great moment in Woody Allen's *Stardust Memories* when his character, movie director Sandy Bates, encounters some aliens. While the director wants to focus on despair and the erosion of the human spirit, the aliens want to talk about comedy, because they prefer his "early funny" films. No matter how much he wants to move on, his audience won't let him.

The bigger problem, in any business, is coming up with the second great idea—the one that builds on the first one and helps transition from just having potential to having a track record. This requires both luck and focus. *That Thing You Do!* written and directed by Tom Hanks, is the story of a 1960s rock and roll band that had neither. Watching it and figuring out what the band did wrong can be a great way of understanding potential and/or existing problems within a business.

For the band, The Wonders, even the first hit has a lot to do with luck. The drummer breaks his arm and is replaced by Guy Patterson (Tom Everett Scott). He takes it upon himself to speed up a ballad, "That Thing You Do," to a rock tempo that gets all the attendees at a talent show on their feet dancing. The movie shows the band's whirlwind rise to the top of the charts, going from country fairs to Hollywood. They end up with a small part in a beach movie and a gig playing on the "Hollywood Television Showcase," all because they have a hit record that is absolutely perfect for the moment, capturing the mood and tempo of the British rock invasion and putting it in all-American clothing.

But you can see the cracks nearly from the beginning. Bandleader Jimmy Mattingly has an inflated sense of his own role in the band. He exercises authority, but doesn't lead. This puts him at odds with the band members, his girlfriend (Liv Tyler), and even the agent (Hanks), who is shepherding them through the perils of stardom. The band's bass player forgets about their shared priorities, meets some Marines, and ends up enlisting and going to Vietnam. Guitarist Lenny, played by the always-funny Steve Zahn, goes to Vegas with a Playboy bunny and ends up married. And Jimmy, thinking he is smarter than their agent, quits the band in a huff rather than do the songs that their agent suggests should be on an album. And suddenly, almost before things have started, it is over. Guy's life actually turns out pretty well—he meets and plays with his idol, jazz musician Del Paxton, and ends up married to Liv Tyler. Not bad as a consolation prize.

I don't suppose he had *That Thing You Do!* in mind at the time, but Amazon CEO Jeff Bezos has said there are four things that have allowed his company to continue to grow and innovate.

- Number one: Obsess over customers. "When given the choice between obsessing over competitors or obsessing over customers, we always obsess over customers," he says. "We like to start with customers and work backwards. If you truly obsess over customers, it will cover a lot of errors." In *That*

Thing You Do! most of the members of the Wonders were more interested in themselves than the audience.

- Number two: Invent. "Anytime we have a problem, we never accept either/or thinking," Bezos says. "We try to figure out a solution that gets both things and that often requires invention. You can invent your way out of any box if you believe if you can." The Wonders weren't continuing to invent, although it wasn't entirely their fault. Once they got onto the show business carousel, duplication and replication became a lot more important than innovation. It's an important business lesson: stay focused.

- Number three: Think long-term. Bezos says, "Any company that wants to focus on customers and put customers first, any company that wants to invent on behalf of customers, has to be willing to think long-term." Bezos says that such thinking often won't pay dividends for the company and its shareholders for five or seven years, though it may pay dividends for customers almost immediately. He also says that thinking long-term "requires...and allows...a willingness to be misunderstood." The Wonders only had short-term goals in mind, which allowed them to be manipulated.

- Number four: "It's always Day One," Bezos says. "There's always more invention in the future, always more customer innovation, new ways to obsess over customers." Every business—or rock and roll band—should have a start-up mentality, especially these days. It keeps you hungry. And motivated.

That Thing You Do! is a perfect little business case study with a bonus—a great soundtrack.

Be the Exception, Not the Rule

If understanding business is difficult, it pales in comparison to understanding dating. Relations between men and women (or other types of couples, for that matter) are never, ever easy.

Modern times have added new wrinkles to dating. What was challenging in the time of Romeo and Juliet, or mysterious to Jane Austen's heroines, is nothing compared to the world of modern technology. Today dating involves a ritual of exchanged e-mails, text messages, Facebook status notes, and even, at times, phone calls.

As one character in *He's Just Not That Into You* explains, dating today involves monitoring multiple technologies just to get disappointed.

It's one of the many terrific lessons in this light, occasionally funny, and altogether forgettable movie. But it deserves our attention because of a single character in the large ensemble: Gigi, played winningly by Ginnifer Goodwin.

Gigi is drowning in the modern dating scene. Her dates end with ambiguous farewells such as "nice to meet you" on a number of communication devices. Days later, Gigi is despondent trying to monitor her home, office, and cell voice mails, plus e-mail, MySpace, and more. And Gigi is always disappointed.

During one failed attempt at getting a second date, Gigi is befriended by a bartender. He has a front-row seat to the current dating game and it's an ugly place. He explains the meaning in all the messages guys give her.

The problem, he says, is that most romantic young women live their lives hoping to be the exception, not the rule. They cling to the notion that a guy who doesn't call will someday re-materialize because they heard of one guy who did so. They trade stories about the guy who could never commit to his long-time girlfriend, only to suddenly propose and become the world's greatest husband.

It's hardly a plot killer to say that by the conclusion of this very predictable movie, every dating convention will turn in favor of the young women and the men will end up on the short end of the stick.

But Gigi's example is worth watching. Gigi loses at love and manages to rebound again and again, and in the process, learns new things about herself and the world around her. In short, she's the person we all need to be.

Gigi's life is full of disappointments, but she never gives in or gives up. She approaches each opportunity with optimism and hope, even as she grows ever wiser from experience. It's a lesson that we learn when we're looking for a job, working for difficult bosses, navigating office politics, or making the tough sale. The emotional attachment that Gigi manages to produce again and again is what makes her so admirable. We suffer with her when she loses and we applaud when she succeeds.

What's important in Gigi's saga is what she learns about being the exception to the rule.

The cynics around Gigi remind her that the rule is where most of us reside. We lose and suffer the losses. In fact, we learn to anticipate the losses and reduce our expectations in advance. But not Gigi. She aims to be the exception.

All businesses should try to emulate Gigi's example. Sure, customers will abuse and abandon us, but that is no excuse to stop good customer service. Sure, co-workers will let us down at times, bosses will disappoint, and trading partners will find someone else. That's when we have to mimic Gigi.

We have to pick ourselves up and approach the next day as though nothing bad happened. We learn from the defeat, but we act as if we have never been beaten. Thomas Edison took many tries before the light bulb worked; Heinz ketchup came after countless failed formulas; Michael Jordan was cut from his high school basketball team.

Defeat is for those who expect to be one of the rules. Success is for the exceptions. And because she is exceptional, we should all want to be like Gigi.

Allow for the Possibility You Are Wrong

B	BRANDING
E	ETHICS

Suggested for all business audiences

THE LATE, GREAT COMEDIAN GEORGE CARLIN once asked about driving: "Why it is that everyone going slower than us is an idiot and everyone going faster is a maniac?" His insight is something all of us believe:

I am always right.

Truth be told, none of us is always right, and we struggle to find a way to admit that we could be a tiny bit wrong. And we hate to have our hypocrisy thrown in our faces, even if the rebuke is deserved.

A powerful lesson about learning to listen comes from the less-than-great movie spun off the HBO mega-hit, *Sex and the City*. The TV series revolved around the love lives and missteps of four devoted and oh-so-different female friends living in New York City. The show's writing was always pretty sharp, the plots could be intriguing, and the characters totally worth following. Especially if you were into shoes and fashion.

Watching *Sex and the City* on television was a guilty pleasure. I know countless women who gathered on Sunday nights to watch new episodes and I know countless men who scoffed at the "chick" show, while stealing glances every chance they could get. (Personally, I was all in for Charlotte, who finds happiness with a man no match for her in appearance. But that's not the point.)

The movie follows the lives of the four heroines a few years after the HBO show ended and gamely tries to manage a longer plot line. We see lustful Samantha trying to fit in on the West Coast in a monogamous relationship, which we know won't last; Charlotte is still loving life as a married mom; Miranda is coping with the balancing act of career and family; and the star, Carrie, is still trying to get her life together with her long time lover Big.

Shoes and fashion still play a huge role, but the lesson from this little film actually comes from the travails facing Miranda.

Now married and living in Brooklyn, Miranda is finding life less than fulfilling. A high-powered lawyer married to a bartender, Miranda shows her struggle to balance her business life with her husband and young son. Her marriage to Steve is fading, as sex, the driving force of the entire television series, becomes an increasingly rare event. The lack of sex is symptomatic of a relationship that is growing more distant.

One day, as Miranda lays out the myriad plans, chores, and duties for the couple, Steve blurts out an admission of infidelity. Miranda explodes and the marriage is over.

Despite repeated attempts by Steve, Miranda will not talk to him, attend counseling, or make any other attempt to save the marriage. If anything, she gets angrier. In one fit of venom, she destroys Carrie's upcoming wedding by filling Big with doubts about marriage.

While the story follows Carrie's collapse at being left at the altar, we watch Miranda stew in her guilt, unable or unwilling to explain what happened between Big and her. When she finally confesses months later, Carrie explodes.

Miranda finds herself in a strange place. She is dying to talk to Carrie, to apologize and to make amends, but Carrie won't see her. Finally Miranda ambushes Carrie in a taxi to beg her forgiveness.

At that point, Carrie delivers the lesson that the movie provides. She asks why Miranda, who won't even talk to her estranged husband, deserves a chance to argue her case to Carrie. Why should Miranda's treatment of Steve be any different than Carrie's treatment of Miranda? Miranda sees the hypocrisy of her approach, which, of course, leads to reconciliation with Steve, repaired friendship with Carrie, and incredible happy endings all around.

But let's recall the lesson. How often has one of us scolded, reprimanded, or done worse to a colleague who behaved as we ourselves had? You can ask the same question of your children, parents, spouse, and friends. How often have we stood on principle against another person without clearly looking at our own behavior? How often have we stood in judgment of others for sins we ourselves have committed? And what have we done about our own faults?

Miranda is a wonderful role model. She doesn't recognize her own hypocrisy. She feels anguish at her own betrayal of Carrie, without ever considering that Steve might feel the same way. But finally, she has that moment of awareness when confronted by Carrie, when she realizes that every conflict has two sides that deserve to be heard.

Arguments in the workplace are a constant and can be a good source of growth for individuals and companies. But like Miranda, we have to realize that none of us are always right. And that even when we *are* right, we need to examine the potential for rapprochement so we can move on, grow, and rebuild.

And maybe throw in a pair of Manolos.

Stiff Competition
Can Eat You Up

B	**BRANDING**
CF	**CUSTOMER FOCUS**

Suggested for all business audiences

NORA EPHRON ISN'T JUST ONE OF THE WITTIEST WRITERS and directors around, with a strong sense of irony and skepticism that infuses much of her work. She also has a very savvy business sense.

Let's consider two of her best movies: *You've Got Mail* and *Julie & Julia*. (Michael already has talked about the wonderful *When Harry Met Sally*, which she wrote but which was directed by Rob Reiner.)

You've Got Mail isn't just a charming romantic comedy starring Tom Hanks and Meg Ryan, at least not when considered within the context of business analysis. No, it actually is a meditation on the challenges facing little retailers when they face the likes of so-called "category killers" such as Home Depot or Barnes & Noble.

The romance of the movie actually hinges on a serious business issue. Meg Ryan's character, Kathleen Kelly, owns a small, charming bookstore on Manhattan's Upper West Side that she inherited from her mother. The bookstore has become a community fixture. The problem is that a Fox Books store is opening up nearby—and Fox Books, an enormous and soulless behemoth, also offers discounts and lattes.

Kathleen reacts too late to the competitive threat. She believes that her history and community connections give her an unassailable advantage, only to find out that there is no such thing. Even longtime customers who love her find themselves seduced by the siren call of Fox Books, and slowly but surely, her business declines to the point where it becomes untenable. She turns to a man she has met only on the Internet for business advice, not knowing that she is confiding in Joe Fox (Hanks), scion of the family that owns the business that is destroying hers. He doesn't know it either, in the beginning...and becomes seriously conflicted when he finds out that his business is wrecking the life of a woman with whom he is falling in love.

Alas, sometimes the battle cannot be won, especially if you are complacent or react too late, which is the central business lesson of *You've Got Mail*. But in business, even the winner doesn't always win. Barnes & Noble had its central business model undercut by Amazon. Blockbuster Video has been undercut by Netflix, which now finds itself being threatened by Redbox kiosks all over America. This is why companies like Amazon and Netflix are constantly looking for ways to keep their business models relevant. Even Walmart has learned the hard way. Although it has been an enormous success in the U.S., it has had big failures and had to pull out of countries like Germany and Korea, and continues to face problems with its stores in Japan.

The key to creating a successful business, even in the face of daunting competition from giants, is to always innovate, to always assume that whatever advantage you have is temporary and that the key to ongoing viability is to constantly look for the next innovation. Tactical thinking helps you deal with the present. Strategic thinking is all about the future. In *You've Got Mail*, Kathleen never makes the transition from tactical to strategic thinking. And she loses. At least professionally.

Julie & Julia, on the other hand, teaches a far more optimistic lesson that is almost the flip side of the one in *You've Got Mail*. In *Julie & Julia*, we see that one can invent a place for oneself in business, or a niche for a business, by finding opportunity where none existed before.

That's what Julia Child (Meryl Streep) does. She realizes that nobody is teaching American housewives in the post-World War II era how to move beyond lowest common denominator supermarket packaged foods. She decides to make French cooking accessible to them, and in the process creates a career for herself and starts a gastronomic revolution that continues even today. That's a great example of innovation, and businesses can learn from it.

It's not that she was looking for a business. Julia is in Paris with her diplomat husband Paul (Stanley Tucci) and is just plain bored. She considers a variety of possibilities, and then realizes that what she loves to do most is eat. She decides to attend the Cordon Bleu cooking school there, where she is the only woman and the only American. Julia is looked at with great skepticism until they discover that she is both fearless and tireless—she will try anything, and she will keep trying until she gets it right. Great lesson here: if you are going to create a business, it always makes sense to do something you love, because that makes it a lot easier when you are doing all the hard work required to become good at it.

This reminds me of Feargal Quinn, the founder of the Superquinn supermarkets in Ireland. Quinn is the quintessential retailer. When he owned Superquinn, he loved nothing more than being in the "shops," chatting with customers, talking to his employees, and being more "shopkeeper" than corporate honcho, even as the business grew. (If you want to read an excellent book about retailing passion, check out his *Crowning the Customer*, one of the best ever written on the subject.)

The importance of both vision and perseverance in any business venture is a constant theme of *Julie & Julia*. It takes a long time for Julia and her co-authors to test all the recipes and write their cookbook. It takes a long time to find a publisher who believes in their vision. But because of the clarity of the vision and their refusal to be dissuaded from their task no matter how tough it becomes, *Mastering the Art of French Cooking* changes the culinary world.

The business world is a tough and unforgiving place. The simple reality is that even if you have vision, passion, patience, and deep enough pockets to hang in there, the very nature of competition can make it almost impossible to survive. That's the law of the jungle—survival of the fittest.

But without the right ingredients at the very beginning, a business has far less of a chance.

MICHAEL'S POV:

Both these movies remind us of the importance of passion and balance. Kathleen Kelly loves children's books and the passion oozes out of her. But no one helps her see that her passion won't be enough. She never actually responds to a competitive threat because she thinks her passion for books is mirrored in her customers. What she forgets is that Value equals more than Passion and her prices are simply too high to keep her in the game.

Julie Powell of *Julie & Julia* has a different problem. Powell is the counterpoint to Julia Child, as half the movie shows Julie in today's world deciding to cook every recipe in Child's cookbook and blog about it. She gets so caught up in her pursuit of cooking Julia Child's recipes that she forgets why she started and why she loves cooking. She melts down completely, endangering everything she holds dear. She reminds us that success and hard work can't be hollow; they must be enjoyed and celebrated. Great workers and managers celebrate moments, their colleagues, and even themselves in much the way that Julia Child celebrated great food.

"*Take Six*"

DRAMA

Protect Your Brand

(Caution: Some of the dialogue quoted is definitely rated "R.")

B	**BRANDING**
	Suggested for all business audiences

Ironically, it takes a hard-core drug dealer to explain in no-doubt-about-it terms why brand equity is to be protected at all costs.

That dramatic moment comes in the middle of *American Gangster*, the drama directed by Ridley Scott, written by Steven Zaillian, and starring Denzel Washington and Russell Crowe. Washington plays Frank Lucas, a Harlem gangster who demonstrates extraordinary entrepreneurial instincts in his drug trade. Lucas cuts out the middle men and goes right to Southeast Asia's Golden Triangle for the high-quality heroin—given the brand name "Blue Magic"—that he sells to people for less money than they can buy inferior heroin from his competition. In fact, if Lucas, a real-life figure, had been using such tactics to sell something legal, they'd be writing textbooks about him.

Lucas finds out that one of his competitors, Leroy Barnes (played by Cuba Gooding, Jr.), has been taking his product, diluting it, and then selling it under the same name. Lucas, to say the least, is not pleased.

Lucas says, "Brand names mean something…Consumers rely on them to know what they're getting. They know the company isn't going to try to fool them with an inferior product. They buy a Ford, they know they're gonna get a Ford. Not a f****n' Datsun. Blue Magic is a brand name; as much a brand name as Pepsi. I own it. I stand behind it. I guarantee it and people know that even if they don't know me any more than they know the chairman of General Foods."

Wow.

Could the CEO of Ford or Pepsi have said it any better?

Maybe Krispy Kreme would have been better off if it had someone with Lucas's sense of brand equity running the joint.

A few years ago, Krispy Kreme was the gold standard of the doughnut business. Known for quality and freshness, it wasn't a brand you could find in a lot of places. But then management saw dollar signs and began an expansion process that eventually resulted in Krispy Kreme doughnuts being sold in every supermarket, convenience store, gas station, and pretty much every kind of retail outlet. Predictably, the quality went down because the doughnuts rarely were as fresh as before. The brand's reputation suffered, and then ran headlong into the Atkins/low carbohydrate movement, which kicked the entire doughnut business in the teeth. The bloom is off the low carb rose, but Krispy Kreme hasn't recovered.

Go back and read Frank Lucas's tirade and ask yourself: if he'd been running Krispy Kreme, would he have done a better job protecting the brand?

I think the answer is pretty obvious.

One of the reasons Frank Lucas was so successful was his ability to fly under the radar of law enforcement. While other drug dealers dressed in the garish outfits associated with pimps, he dressed like an accountant and avoided conspicuous consumption that would attract attention.

Lucas explains his aversion to showy clothes: "That's a clown suit. That's a costume, with a big sign on it that says 'Arrest me.' You understand? You're too loud, you're making too much noise. Listen to me, the loudest one in the room is the weakest one in the room."

In other words, protect the brand.

When Lucas's fall begins, it is because his beautiful wife buys him a full-length fur coat and insists that he wear it to a boxing match. The detectives who are engaged in a stakeout at the match notice him for the first time, and wonder who he is, and that's when the investigation into his activities begins. That investigation eventually leads to Lucas's arrest and incarceration. It isn't much later in the movie that Lucas actually burns the coat, realizing that a brief moment of weakness—a moment when he was thinking about something other than his brand's equity—could bring about his downfall.

In its own way, *American Gangster* is very much a prototypically American story, and its protagonist offers an important business lesson about the value of a brand. The product is heroin, but it could have been about doughnuts.

THE SHAWSHANK REDEMPTION (1994)

Get Busy Living

P	PLANNING
	Suggested for all business audiences

FEW MOVIES TELL THEIR STORY with more mixed emotions than the wonderful prison drama, *The Shawshank Redemption*. Based on a novella by Stephen King, *Shawshank* tells the incredible tale of a banker wrongly imprisoned for the murder of his wife who finds a way to use his skills to survive a brutal prison. In the end, he uses the skills he learned inside the walls of Shawshank prison to emerge as a new man in every way possible.

The movie soars thanks to great acting, especially the spectacular performances of Tim Robbins and Morgan Freeman. It has a great story with fascinating moral dilemmas encountered by the protagonists. The prisoners have spirited debates about the lines between right and wrong.

In one ongoing debate, Andy Dufresne (Robbins) and Ellis Boyd "Red" Redding (Freeman) argue whether hope itself is a good or bad thing in prison. Dufresne, the wrongfully imprisoned prisoner, says it keeps him going. Redding, the hardened and properly convicted prisoner, argues the opposite. He says hope can drive a man crazy behind walls, and he urges Dufresne to drop it.

The lesson, however, comes not from this debate, but rather, from a line repeated throughout the movie. At various times, whether facing the reality of prison, the potential of parole, or even life outside the walls, the choice is simple.

Get busy living or get busy dying.

Ask yourself which choice you make in your business. Are you building for the future, investing in your people, your company, and yourself? Are you reading and learning, constantly trying to grow? Are you finding ways to challenge yourself to take on the next task and get ready for what you cannot even see?

In short, are you busy living?

Or are you, like so many sadly are, busy only getting ready to die? We know too many businesses that seem to be approaching their days like a football team with the ball and the clock running down. They "take a knee" again and again, forgoing the opportunity to do something new. They pass on the moment and sit pat. They find reasons to stop investing in their people, products and customers. They scoff at new trends, preferring to do things the way they have always been done.

And invariably, they are swept under when the unexpected happens. In short, they are busy dying.

Some of life's problems are murky to figure out, such as whether hope is worthwhile or dangerously foolhardy. But some issues are just as simple as they come:

Get busy living or get busy dying.

KEVIN'S POV:

In the food retailing business, something about which I have spent a lot of time writing over the past two decades, there has been tumult in recent years from technological changes, such as online shopping, that threaten traditional business models.

Some senior executives have not gotten busy living. They refuse to embrace some of the challenges and opportunities that technology creates, preferring to count the days until they can retire and leave those decisions to other people.

You know how you can tell who these people are? When they send you an email, you see that their assistant or secretary actually is sending it. They say they use email, but what that really means is that their emails are printed out for them to read.

How can such a person expect to understand or market to a culture that uses Twitter, Facebook, YouTube, and more?

The simple answer is that they can't. And they can't because they're not busy living.

Make Sure Your Words Count

E	ETHICS
L	LEADERSHIP
Suggested for all business audiences	

WE'VE ALL SAT IN MEETINGS where a top executive gets up and delivers a speech that is so uninspiring and so lacking in credibility, the first thing we do when we get back to our desks is make sure our resumes are up to date and call an executive search firm.

I used to know some guys like that. You just knew that when they made either of the following two statements—"things are turning around" or "this is the last of the layoffs"—that things were about to get a lot worse and/or heads were going to roll. It got to the point that we knew these guys were lying whenever they moved their lips.

Now, I'm not sure these executives meant any harm. They may have even believed what they were saying for a few brief moments, or thought they were doing the right thing when they tried unsuccessfully to shield us from reality. What they didn't understand was this:

Words matter.

They really do. There's no such thing as "just words." Actions don't always speak louder than words. It is through our words that we signal our intentions, that we establish our goals, that we move people to believe and follow us. And when the words ring hollow, people lose faith and leadership is doomed.

Hoosiers happens to be one of the best sports movies ever made. But it also is a movie that teaches us the power of words. In *Hoosiers*, Coach Norman Dale, played by Gene Hackman, finds himself coaching basketball in a small rural Indiana high school in 1952 after a tumultuous and controversial career. Hackman gets to deliver some of the best-written motivational speeches in the movies. Ever.

And most importantly, he makes speeches that are appropriate to the moment.

He delivers a speech to his players before the regional finals, telling them that, in his heart, he has no expectation of winning the game: "If you put your effort and concentration into playing to your potential, to be the best that you can be, I don't care what the scoreboard says at the end of the game. In my book we're gonna be winners."

He knows exactly what to say to "Shooter" Flatch, the town drunk played by Dennis Hopper, who also happens to be a basketball wizard. He asks him to be his assistant coach, on the condition that he stops drinking. It is an offer at redemption that Flatch finds impossible to turn down.

When talking to Jimmy Chitwood, a fabulously talented player who has chosen not to play basketball despite pressure from friends and locals, he takes the opposite tack. "You know, in the ten years that I coached, I never met anybody who wanted to win as badly as I did," Dale says. "I'd do anything I had to do to increase my advantage. Anybody who tried to block the pursuit of that advantage, I'd just push 'em out of the way. Didn't matter who they were, or what they were doing. But that was then. You have special talent, a gift. Not the school's, not the townspeople, not the team's, not Myra Fleener's, not mine. It's yours, to do with what you choose. Because that's what I believe, I can tell you this: I don't care if you play on the team or not."

Needless to say, he plays.

At the end of the movie, when the team actually makes the state championships, he walks the team into the gymnasium where the final game will be played. It's a basketball palace, far bigger and more impressive than the tiny high school gym they are used to. What does Coach Dale do? He takes out a tape measure and has the boys measure the height of the basket and the distance to the foul line, and points out that it is precisely the same as back home. Don't worry about the size of the gym, he says, just play your game.

And, when sketching out the final play of a game in which he needs the shortest and least talented kid on the team to sink two foul shots before the team gets the ball back, he says "when" he makes the foul shots, not "if"—establishing without question his high level of confidence in *all* of the players.

Words matter.

Many years ago, I was coaching a Little League team that, improbably, got to the finals. (Extremely improbably. Trust me on this one.) When we got to the field on that hot June Sunday afternoon, I gathered the team around me, pulled out a tape measure, and showed them that even for the final game of the season, the distance from the pitcher's mound to home plate, and the distance from base to base, was exactly the same as it was the rest of the season. "So don't worry about it being the final game," I told them. "If you put your effort and concentration into playing to your potential, to be the best that you can be, I don't care what the scoreboard says at the end of the game. In my book we're gonna be winners."

That's right. I stole Coach Dale's speech, almost word for word. The parents on the sidelines couldn't believe it…in fact, they were cracking up because they all knew exactly what movie I was stealing from. But the kids nodded, solemnly. They got it.

Those little kids, by the way, played their hearts out. Unfortunately, we also got our butts kicked.

But I was proud of them, and I was glad that at one particular moment, I'd been able to turn to a movie and find the narrative I needed to tell those kids what they needed to hear.

Challenge What You Know

E	ETHICS
L	LEADERSHIP
Suggested for all business audiences	

PREJUDICE IN ANY FORM CAN BE CRIPPLING. If you and your associates think you know the answers before you know the questions, odds are the business won't last long.

In the Heat of the Night begins with a murder outside a small Mississippi town in the mid-1960s. As the police survey the murder scene, the chief orders his men to look for any strangers passing through town. The first place they check is the railroad station and within moments, an arrest is made.

Inside the station is Virgil Tibbs, and he's instantly a suspect for two reasons: he's a stranger and he's black. Once in custody, the police find a piece of incriminating evidence. The dead man was a wealthy industrialist and his usually fat wallet is missing. Tibbs is carrying a significant amount of cash.

When the police chief questions Tibbs about the money, the truth is stunning. Tibbs is a policeman from Philadelphia and the money is his. He has a badge and in short order, he has his captain on the phone supporting his story.

Chief Gillespie, played by Rod Steiger (an Oscar winning role in an Oscar winning movie), is a man shaped by the prejudice of his job, his location, and his time. To him, the arrest of a black man who is a stranger to his town makes sense. In fact, when he first questions Tibbs, played equally brilliantly by Sidney Poitier, his questions have nothing to do with the means, motive, or opportunity. He simply suggests that Tibbs will feel a whole lot better confessing the crime.

Tibbs is also shaped by prejudice. He understands the realities of the South and has made his escape. When his chief from up North suggests he help the local cops solve the crime, Tibbs, who is a specialist in homicides, vehemently disagrees. He has no more use for the Mississippi police than they have for him. But he stays to help solve the murder.

Both Gillespie and Tibbs think they know all the answers before they even know the questions. Chief Gillespie makes three arrests for the murder, convinced each time he has the right suspect. His cops arrest a local man, Harvey, who was caught with the dead man's wallet. Gillespie is sure Harvey is the killer until Tibbs explains that the killer must be left-handed and the suspect is not. Then Gillespie arrests one of his own officers who was guilty of nothing more than concealing a detail from Tibbs and making a bank deposit.

But Tibbs shows his prejudice, too. Although he approaches the case with a thirst for evidence, he clearly has a theory. The murdered man was planning to open a factory in the town. The factory would give the local black population good jobs and would upset the town's long-held power structure.

Tibbs and Gillespie pay a visit to a local plantation owned by an old money patrician. After a confrontational scene, Tibbs tells Gillespie to give him time to bring the "fat cat down."

This time, Gillespie teaches the lesson. He tells Tibbs that he is just as prejudiced as everyone else in the town. Tibbs realizes Gillespie is correct. He steps back, rethinks all the evidence he's gathered, and finally narrows in on the correct killer.

Prejudice in business comes in so many ways. There are racial, ethnic, and gender preferences that have led far too many companies to make dreadful mistakes, to ignore people or great potential, and to even ignore markets. Unfortunately, human nature indicates these problems won't go away anytime soon.

But prejudice comes in many other forms. There are countless business examples of great ideas that were dismissed because they came from the wrong people, and ideas that never took fruition because they didn't seem quite right.

If you look at the radical start-ups in any industry, you'll see ideas that somehow the establishment was too prejudiced to see: Southwest Airlines, Apple personal computers, Enterprise Car Rental, Fuji high-speed film, Ben & Jerry's ice cream. In nearly every case you'll find the same thing: someone missed the big idea because all their training, all their background, and all their experience taught them to view a problem one way. They never realized there was an option.

In the Heat of the Night is one of many films that explores the negative power of pre-conceived notions. *Legally Blonde* and *Beauty and the Beast* do the same thing. The wonderful book and hit Broadway musical *Wicked* plows this ground by forcing us to see the time-honored story of *The Wizard of Oz* from the perspective of the wicked witch.

The lesson is always the same. Every story has another side. Like Tibbs and Gillespie, we need to stretch, learn, and grow. We need to encourage alternative views and nurture different points of view. We need to accept that what we absolutely know to be true might sometimes be completely wrong. And like Tibbs and Gillespie, who end the movie as begrudging friends, we need to understand that we can grow stronger from the experience.

Otherwise, we might arrest the wrong suspect again and again, without ever getting close to solving the crime.

Art and Commerce Can Co-Exist

B	BRANDING
CF	CUSTOMER FOCUS
L	LEADERSHIP
Suggested for all business audiences	

IN MANY BUSINESSES, THERE IS THE STRUGGLE between art and commerce, between the visionaries and the bottom line. In movies, this battle is well illustrated in the movie *Big Night*, which was one of the most successful independent movies released during the mid-nineties.

Written by Stanley Tucci and Joseph Tropiano, and co-directed by Tucci and Campbell Scott, *Big Night* is a perfect little jewel—its beauty is in its precision, its understatement, and ultimately, in the emotional connection it makes to the audience.

Set in a small New Jersey town during the 1950s, *Big Night* is about two brothers, Primo (Tony Shalhoub) and Secondo (Tucci), who own and operate an Italian restaurant. Primo, the chef, is a man in love with the art of cooking. His goal is to serve his customers "real" Italian food that will awaken their souls as well as their taste buds. "To eat good food is to be close to God," he says. He is enraged one night when he makes perfect seafood risotto for one patron, who then asks for spaghetti and meatballs on the side. Describing a competitor, he says, "Do you know what happens in that restaurant every night? RAPE! RAPE! The rape of cuisine." This is a guy who takes cooking seriously.

Secondo is the businessman, and he understands that when people think about Italian food, they think of spaghetti and meatballs and garlic bread, and that a successful Italian restaurant has to offer these things (it's the 1950s, not today). Secondo thinks the restaurant is there to serve people what they want and make a buck. His brother believes fervently that his mission is to educate and enlighten people.

Of course, if the restaurant could exist in spite of—or even because of—this creative tension, the world might be a better place. But it can't, and it is close to going out of business. Another restaurant nearby is booming, precisely because the owner has no ambition to the artistry that is practiced by Primo and reluctantly respected by Secondo.

The brothers begin to prepare for the possibility that Louie Prima, a famous bandleader of the day, will visit their restaurant, propel it into the headlines, and all but guarantee its future success. It is not giving away too much of the plot, I think, to suggest that there is a little bit of *Waiting For Godot* here. The importance of the celebrity endorsement, and whether it will be earned with seafood risotto or spaghetti and meatballs, is at the crux of the movie.

One of the great lessons of *Big Night* is that there is no good guy or bad guy; no argument is presented in such a way that it has an unfair advantage in gaining the audience's sympathy. Both brothers have a point, and each respects the other's position.

In the early 1990s, I traveled to Boulder, Colorado to interview one of the founders of the Boulder Brewing Company. This was early in the days of the brewpub/microbrewery phenomenon, and I was anxious to see how the company could compete with the likes of Anheuser-Busch and Colorado neighbor Coors with a product that was often called "the dirty beer" because it had sediment at the bottom of the bottle.

"We are going to succeed because we make a terrific product, and because we are investing in it," I was told in that long-ago interview, as the beer entrepreneur gestured around at the shiny new brewing facility he and his investors had built.

And then he said something that I will never forget: "We're not like that brewing company back East that isn't even really a brewing company. They're spending all their money on marketing and are letting other companies brew their beer using a special recipe. We're going to succeed in the long term because we are investing in the product, not the hype."

That "brewing company back East," of course, was a little company called The Boston Beer Company, and it made a beer called Samuel Adams.

There, in real life, you had a classic conflict between art and commerce. It isn't hard to figure out which side won. When was the last time you had a Boulder Beer? I hasten to note that as of this writing, the Boulder Brewing Company is still in business, and I am not maligning the founders, the management, or the vision. But they underestimated the power of actually getting people—lots of people—to try their product.

The lesson in *Big Night* is that there needs to be compromise between art and commerce. While art, or at least whatever passes for art in your business, needs to be achieved or at least aimed for, there is no art that really matters without customers to appreciate it and, yes, pay for it. So respect and appreciate both camps in your business venture. In business, art needs commerce to flourish. On the other hand, businesses can use artistic principles to distinguish themselves from competitors.

At the end of *Big Night*, there is a scene that is played almost in silence, as one brother makes for the other a perfect omelet. But it shows the movie's great appreciation of both characters and both sides of the debate that it allows Secondo to make the omelet for Primo.

Even a sales guy can have a soul and the capacity for art.

MICHAEL'S POV:

The battle waged between the brothers is a battle you see in many companies. Businesses can avoid it if they approach the problem differently. The task facing Primo and Secondo was to educate their patrons to eat more authentic Italian food. In the process the restaurant would have built a point of differentiation. Many good businesses do this, changing our expectation of value and our willingness to pay more. Consider how cell phone companies are constantly teaching us about new applications and services that no one knew they needed until strong marketing made them a "must have." Art and commerce can mix beautifully and profitably.

BROADCAST NEWS (1987)
GOOD NIGHT, AND GOOD LUCK (2005)

Know the Value of Ethics and Truth

E	ETHICS
Suggested for all business audiences	

The films *Broadcast News* and *Good Night, and Good Luck* offer two different cinematic views of the television news business, set more than three decades apart. They look at the same issues through very different prisms.

Broadcast News is a wonderful and highly entertaining example of how it is possible for companies to value the wrong qualities in their employees. Written and directed by James L. Brooks, this movie shows how following the wrong values can lead to a moral and ethical decline.

The pivotal character is Aaron Altman, played by Albert Brooks as a neurotic but brilliant on-camera correspondent for a network news organization. While Altman is an expert reporter and writer, he yearns to be an anchorman because that's the pinnacle of success in the network news business. Just being a great reporter isn't good enough in a world where presentation skills are placed above the ability to get at the truth.

And so, when Altman is offered the chance to anchor a weekend edition of the nightly news, he leaps at it, and as anyone who has seen the movie will recall, experiences on-camera the funniest case of flop sweat ever broadcast. It is so bad that some viewers call in, worried that he is having a heart attack. Propelled by his own ego, he's been put in the wrong job by a system that puts a premium on qualities he doesn't possess.

Tom Grunick, played by William Hurt with exactly the right amount of stupidity leavened by charm, is the opposite of Altman. He isn't very smart, but he looks great on-camera and knows how to connect with the audience, even if he has to take some ethical shortcuts to do so. He may not know how to write a story, or even know what is important about a story, but he knows how to present a story, which is why he's on the fast track for the anchor's chair.

To give Grunick credit, he actually knows what he doesn't know, which offers him a kind of moral redemption in the mind of the audience. There's a great moment in the movie where Grunick asks Altman, "What do you do when your real life exceeds your dreams?" and Altman offers the perfect response: "Keep it to yourself."

Jane Craig is the news producer who finds herself both personally and professionally torn between Altman and Grunick. As portrayed by Holly Hunter at her vulnerable best, Craig knows that Altman is a superior newsman to Grunick, but realizes that Grunick is the future, albeit one she is repulsed by. And though she is Altman's best friend, at the same time, she is drawn to Grunick's charm.

Broadcast News offers a wonderful narrative that companies can use to define the edges of ethical behavior, and to help flesh out what is valuable in their own organizations. It also sounds some significant warning notes, as when Altman tries to point out Grunick's shortcomings to Craig:

"I know you care about him. I've never seen you like this about anyone, so please don't take it wrong when I tell you that I believe that Tom, while a very nice guy, is the Devil…What do you think the Devil is going to look like if he's around? He will look attractive and he will be nice and helpful and he will get a job where he influences a great God-fearing nation and he will never do an evil thing...he will just, bit by little bit, lower standards where they are important...And he'll get all the great women."

That's a powerful statement because it cautions against being too attracted to the easy solution, the attractive alternative, the convenient excuse. These are choices that every business and every business leader/manager are faced with at some point in their lives.

As a counterpoint, consider *Good Night, and Good Luck*, the excellent film directed and co-written by George Clooney about the conflict between the legendary newsman Edward R. Murrow and Senator Joseph McCarthy (R-Wisconsin). The film portrays Murrow and CBS News as paradigms of uncommon courage. Senator McCarthy was holding hearings in which he was crusading against Communists and destroying innocent people's lives, and virtually the entire nation feared even intimations that they might once have been sympathetic to members of the Communist party. By taking the fight directly to McCarthy and showing that he was using fear to stifle political debate and discourse, Murrow (David Strathairn) and his producer Fred Friendly (Clooney) put their careers—not to mention CBS—at risk, with the belief that the truth eventually would win out.

It was highly unlikely in the early 1950s that anyone would actually utter these words on national television, but there Murrow was, looking at the camera and saying:

"We must not confuse dissent from disloyalty. We must remember always that accusation is not proof, and that conviction depends upon evidence and due process of law...This is no time for men who oppose Senator McCarthy's methods to keep silent or for those who approve. We can deny our heritage and our history but we cannot escape responsibility for the result...We proclaim ourselves, as indeed we are, the defenders of freedom wherever it still exists in the world. But we cannot defend freedom abroad by deserting it at home."

This is a case of confronting the devil, not being seduced by him, and *Good Night, and Good Luck* puts moral courage front and center. The movie points out that often the person who challenges conventional wisdom is the person of real value to a business. This isn't a bad lesson to teach members of any organization.

AMADEUS (1984)

Travel the Road
Less Taken

IMAGINE THIS SCENARIO: You are sitting around your office/store/factory/workplace when someone makes a radical suggestion—an entirely new way of doing something you have always done. What is the likely response of those around the room?

A. People take turns pointing out "we don't do things that way."

B. People take turns belittling the idea.

C. People silently ignore the idea, and afterwards find time
   to bash it and the person who suggested it.

D. People charge out to embrace the new path.

If your workplaces are like most we have experienced, the odds are that "D" is the least popular answer. It's why some of the best innovations have come at times from people who tried to advance them in-house, only to be ignored. For example, there was the manager of a Ben Franklin general merchandise store who proposed a new way of running a retail operation. The employee, named Sam, wanted to sell goods at the lowest possible price to the public. The poor guy left his job in frustration. The company he founded—Walmart—put his old employer (and lots of other companies) out of business.

Consider the iPod. It wasn't the first personal music player, but it revolutionized the way we listen to music. Its sleek design and inexpensive music downloads has led to widespread adulation of the device.

It's hard to find a better and more enjoyable movie about the battle between the radical and the status quo than the brilliant *Amadeus*. Based on a Broadway play by Peter Shaffer, *Amadeus* is a fictionalized account of the life of Wolfgang Amadeus Mozart, with a heavy focus on the composer's decline and death.

What makes the story so engaging is how it is told: through the eyes of Antonio Salieri, a colleague and rival of Mozart in the court of the Austrian Emperor. As the story makes clear, Salieri was by far the more successful of the two. He was the favorite of the Emperor, Vienna, and the city's leading citizens. But Salieri knew that Mozart, portrayed as an undisciplined, tormented vulgarian, possessed true genius.

Salieri drives Mozart to ruin. But Salieri lives long enough to see his own music and skills forgotten, and Mozart's legacy grow. In one painful scene, Salieri watches his one chance to collaborate with Mozart, and therefore ensure his own legacy, disappear because of his past deeds.

While the movie clearly packs a powerful lesson about the price of envy and jealousy, the real business story has to do with innovation.

We find a lesson in the repeated battle between Mozart's attempts at creativity through new and different musical ideas and the resistance of the status quo that seemed determined to stop him at every turn. When we first meet Mozart, his brusque manner is quickly established, but so is his musical greatness. Asked to compose an opera for the Emperor, Mozart rejects the usual subjects of standard opera. Rather, he selects a libretto set in a brothel and proposes staging it in German rather than the usual Italian.

The keepers of the status quo are aghast, but Mozart prevails with the support of the Emperor. However, that support is only temporary, because the elaborate work proves too complex for the Emperor's taste. While he praises Mozart's work as ingenious, he also suggests that somehow it contains too many notes, a complaint young Mozart is stunned to hear.

Mozart's battles with Salieri rage on. When he incorporates dancing into one opera, he is told that he violates the rules and must remove the music that plays during the dance. Mozart's choice of stories is routinely questioned, as is his staging, and even his ability to teach music. In short, everything that makes him a genius is treated with disdain.

The plot of *Amadeus* relies on all these elements, but places all the blame on Salieri, who is portrayed as a vindictive foe, bent on destroying Mozart because the younger composer casually possesses all the gifts he wishes for himself. No doubt there are people in the workplace who are equally moved by jealousy and envy to stop what is best for their company in the name of holding their own position.

But *Amadeus* shows us much more. Despite the clear recognition of his superiority, no one comes to the side of the composer. Rather, the status quo wins again and again, as is often the case. Many companies embrace the status quo and do not give true innovators like Mozart the opportunity to invigorate their companies. In the movie, Mozart dies. Unlike Sam Walton and Steve Jobs, he was not able to rise above the status quo and popularize his radical ideas in his lifetime.

It's a lesson well worth considering: are you part of the status quo or are you a Mozart? Are you Ben Franklin stores or are you Walmart? The honest answer may disappoint you. Few among us are Mozarts, but if you seek excellence in your business, you won't be satisfied with the way things have always been done.

Find the Magic

B	BRANDING
CF	**CUSTOMER FOCUS**

Suggested for all business audiences

THIS MOVIE IS A SENTIMENTAL CHOICE for me because it concerns a subject that I love—wine.

Now, to be clear, I am no oenophile. I wouldn't even go so far to describe myself as any sort of an expert. Far from it. I'm an enthusiast. I have no idea what a tannin is, but it doesn't matter. In *Bottle Shock*, Alan Rickman, playing Steven Spurrier, a British wine merchant trying to establish his business in Paris, puts it this way: "Wine is sunlight held together by water." That's pure poetry and passion. I can't explain it, or understand it, but somehow, I get it.

There are business lessons to be learned from *Bottle Shock*, which is a generally under-appreciated movie about the dawn of the California wine industry. In 1976, Spurrier is sponsoring a blind tasting event to pit California wines against French vintages. At that time, California wines were regarded poorly, and the French dominated the wine world with an arrogance and snobbery that didn't even leave open the possibility that decent wines, not to mention extraordinary wines, could be produced elsewhere.

Bottle Shock is a highly fictionalized version of the events leading up to Spurrier's tasting event, at which California wines defeated the French wines, even though the judges were all French. The American wine business is seen through the eyes of Jim Barrett (Bill Pullman), a former lawyer who is struggling to make his Chateau Montelena vineyard a success despite daunting odds. Barrett is convinced that he can make wines on a par with the French, but it is an expensive, exhausting, and frustrating process that puts him at odds with his hippie son Bo (Chris Pine) and a local man, Gustavo Brambila (Freddie Rodriguez), who has wine in his blood. Barrett has grown so bitter that he doesn't see Spurrier's taste test as an opportunity; rather, he is suspicious that he's being set up for yet another humiliation.

One could look at the way Barrett operates his vineyard in *Bottle Shock* and probably find all sorts of business lessons: 1) the dangers of doing business with family, 2) the problem with being autocratic, and 3) why one has to be careful about being mortgaged up to one's eyeballs.

But that's not what I see when I watch *Bottle Shock*. I see people filled with passion for what they do, and how that passion helps them get past the problems and pitfalls.

What drives Barrett's business, and pretty much every character in the movie, is the passion that he feels for his product. Despite the obstacles, there are moments throughout the film when people sip from a glass of wine, and are, at least for a moment, transported. They remember that they are not working so much for the process, but rather for that moment when a person will taste the wine and be transformed. "You'll tell your children and grandchildren about this chardonnay," Jim Barrett thunders at one point in the movie…and who would doubt him?

At some level, it might seem easier to feel such passion for the wine and food business, as opposed, say, to the hardware business. I'm not sure that's true, though. I think that the person who works in the hardware store is able to find the poetry in a hammer and nail, understanding that he is making it possible for people to build and create and be self-sufficient. That the person who works in a dry cleaner is able to see the romance in freshly laundered clothes and what that may mean to the person who is going out on a date or going to a job interview. I hope that the person working in a drug store sees not just medicines and beauty care items, but products that help people look and feel well. That's one of the things that made Starbucks a success—it wasn't selling coffee, but was offering the poetry of a "third place" experience.

I'm lucky. I love words and ideas, and I get to traffic in them pretty much every day. When I see people who are unhappy in their work, or not taking real joy in it, I see people who have lost touch with the poetry and romance of their occupation.

So there's the business lesson of *Bottle Shock*. Whether you are an owner, a manager, or an employee, an important part of your job ought to be identifying the magic and communicating it, both to the people who work for you and to your customers.

Mark Twain once wrote, "What work I have done I have done because it has been play. If it had been work I shouldn't have done it." That isn't easy to achieve, but it is a worthy goal.

Find the magic in your business. It may not always have the romance and poetry of a great chardonnay or pinot noir. But it will still be delicious.

ALL THE PRESIDENT'S MEN (1976)
NETWORK (1976)

Take the Long View

RB	RULE BREAKERS
E	ETHICS
L	LEADERSHIP
Suggested for all business audiences	

THE YEAR 1976 PRODUCED TWO FILMS with vastly different views of the media business—one optimistic, one almost dismayingly cynical. The bad news, of course, is that the concerns voiced by the latter have been borne out. But both movies offer valuable business lessons.

All the President's Men is the outstanding Alan J. Pakula film based on the bestselling book by Bob Woodward and Carl Bernstein of the *Washington Post*. It tells about the reporting of the Watergate story at a time when most news people were either not paying attention or were downright skeptical. Nobody at that time could conceive of a series of events that would force the resignation of a U.S. president, but that is precisely what happened, mostly because of investigative reporting done by two dogged young journalists.

The word "dogged" is an important one in the context of business lessons. *All the President's Men* is a detective story, and it was critically important to the success of Woodward and Bernstein's investigation that they remained tightly focused on the work at hand. Their superiors, chiefly Executive Editor Ben Bradlee (played by Jason Robards), gave them room to work and minimized the distractions, while always holding the reporters accountable for the accuracy of their work. This is a good model for how any boss should empower employees—keep them focused, give them room, demand results.

In addition, *All the President's Men* is a good example of smart staffing. At the beginning of the movie, Woodward (Robert Redford) and Bernstein (Dustin Hoffman) hardly know each other and certainly don't like each other; Bernstein is dismayed to find out that Woodward, a former Navy officer, is actually a Republican. They have very different styles of working, with Bernstein being the better natural writer and Woodward being the stronger reporter. And yet, they complement each other. The work is actually more effective for being crafted by two unique personalities with different perspectives.

All the President's Men reminds us that in business, as in journalism, sometimes failure is a step on the path to greater achievement. At one point in the investigation, Woodward and Bernstein get a key fact wrong, not out of malice, but because they ask a question the wrong way and don't understand the context of the answer. That mistake opens them to attack by the Nixon White House. They redouble their efforts, keep working the story, and eventually cause the Watergate hearings to take place, leading to Nixon's resignation from office.

Let's reiterate the business lessons from *All the President's Men*:
- Stay focused.
- Give employees room to do their jobs.
- Build a strong team by putting together strong personalities that complement each other.
- Failure builds character and makes achievement all the sweeter.

All the President's Men looks at one of the great journalistic success stories. In contrast, *Network* is a scathing satire that looks into the journalistic abyss. The film, written by Paddy Chayefsky and directed by Sidney Lumet, postulates a world in which television news is about ratings and personalities, not journalism and accuracy.

Yes, that's right. *Network* may be one of the greatest predictive movies ever made. In fact, it is so spot-on that when you watch it today, knowing it was made more than three decades ago, you marvel at Chayefsky's clairvoyance.

Peter Finch plays Howard Beale, a network anchorman who is fired for low ratings. He reacts to the news of his firing by ranting and raving on the air that he's going to commit suicide on camera. That shoots his ratings up, and he gets a reprieve; in fact, he is encouraged to rant and rave as much as he wants. He exhorts his viewers to throw open their windows and yell, "I'm mad as hell, and I'm not going to take it anymore!" The loonier he gets, the more the network loves him.

His news director and best friend, Max Schumacher (William Holden), is replaced by the manipulative and ratings-minded Diana Christensen (Faye Dunaway), who sees only dollar signs. She has no concern for the loss of network credibility or Beale's eroding emotional stability. The end is tragic and inevitable once events have been set in motion by people who have little if any ethical compass.

Watch *Network* from beginning to end, and see how most of the people in power make the wrong decision time after time because they are focused on short-term results rather than long-term business equity. Forget about the broader ethical and journalistic implications: can we actually trust news programs that are more entertainment than news, and that are crafted for ratings rather than illumination? These guys are making lousy business decisions that eventually bring down the network. The closing image of the movie is a newscast that actually dissolves into irrelevance, just so much noise.

That's the nightmare scenario in any business: irrelevance. It's why *Network* is a terrific movie to watch and discuss with subordinates, as you look for parallels to your own business. We all want to think our companies can take a longer view rather than buckle under the pressure of short-term profits. Giving employees the chance to work the story, to build the case, as Woodward and Bernstein do in *All the President's Men*, yields a result that makes history. Making decisions on the strength of today's ratings alone, as they do in *Network*, destroys everyone.

THE GODFATHER (1972)

This is Business, Not Personal

E	ETHICS
L	LEADERSHIP
P	PLANNING
Suggested for all business audiences	

If you could watch only one movie that models business, management, and competitive concerns, offering lessons and insights to leaders and managers about what to do and, just as important, what not to do, rent or buy *The Godfather*, the remarkable Francis Ford Coppola movie about a New York crime family in the post–World War II era. Even today, almost four decades after its release, *The Godfather* continues to be cited in most polls as one of the best movies ever made. It resonates far beyond the movie screen.

Not long ago, in a *New York Times* profile of Afghanistan president Hamid Karzai, one United Nation official said that he should think of his regime as *The Godfather, Part II* and strive to go legitimate. No word on whether Karzai actually has seen *The Godfather*…but he should.

To sum up the essential business lessons of *The Godfather*, we decided to share this chapter and offer a running commentary on the film akin to what you might hear in the "special features" section of a DVD.

MICHAEL: This movie delivers from its opening moment. There's the poor undertaker Bonasera needing a favor to avenge his daughter's beating. He comes to petition Don Corleone on the day of his daughter's wedding, a day on which Vito by tradition cannot refuse a request. But Vito is put out. "I can't remember the last time you invited me to your house for a cup of coffee...you never wanted my friendship. You were afraid to be in my debt," Vito says.

The business lesson is clear. Build relationships in good times, not when you have a problem. This is something we've seen throughout the years, often between businesses and the media. Companies decline to cultivate the relationship in good times and suddenly have no connections when facing bad publicity or charges.

Like Bonasera, they don't pro-actively build relations.

KEVIN: It's like that old line: Be nice to people you meet on the way up, because you are likely to meet them again on the way down.

Beyond the issue of personal relationships, these scenes from *The Godfather* point out that decisions have consequences. You make certain alliances in business, and other avenues are going to be closed off to you. That's what happens when Bonasera comes to Vito to ask for vengeance. Business decisions almost never are made in a vacuum.

I think Vito shows great management skill in how he deals with Bonasera. He could have rejected him outright or humiliated him. But instead, he just expresses a kind of pained regret at how their relationship has developed. This reaction encourages Bonasera to take the next step, which is to invest emotionally in the Don and his business enterprise. Corleone maintains the veneer of civility, which ensures that the people who work for him, even tangentially, have skin in the game. That's always the best way to deal with employees.

Of course, sometimes tough love works best and we see it in how Vito deals with the singer, Johnny Fontaine. Vito berates him for whining about his career mishaps, and then promises to do what he can to help, as long as Johnny behaves like a man.

Great management advice here: You can't treat all your employees the same way.

MICHAEL: That point is actually made throughout the wedding scenes, as Vito entertains four visitors and each one has a different Godfather experience. The baker Nazorine gets a friendly meeting befitting his long relationship with Vito. Johnny gets yelled at and Bonasera gets a lesson. But most strikingly is how Vito receives Luca Brasi, his scary and monstrous hit man. Brasi needs a soft, gentle, and focused audience. Vito stands and never breaks eye contact. For Brasi, noisy children are quieted.

Vito understands that different relationships must be worked differently; that he must be a different boss to many different personalities. It's an incredible challenge in management and one that great bosses learn. Some associates perform best with tough direction and some with wide leeway. And different situations call for different types of communication, too. Vito shows it all.

I read a piece in *Sports Illustrated* about the fabulous Cincinnati Reds teams of the 1970s that provided an interesting parallel. Manager Sparky Anderson told the team that superstars like Pete Rose and Johnny Bench were allowed far more leeway that the rest of the team because their past earned them that respect. Younger players got very different treatment.

A lack of managerial sensitivity to individual needs is portrayed in *The Godfather*. Sonny, the hot-tempered oldest son, treats everyone the same and rarely with courtesy. Sonny is the type of boss we all dread having.

KEVIN: In any good organization, loyalty has to go both ways. The people at the top have to be loyal to the rank and file or they have no right to expect loyalty—that seems to be a central business tenet of how Don Corleone runs his organization. And the business is threatened only when loyalty starts to erode. (And maybe vice-versa.)

The Godfather uses two scenes to make its next important business point: why you never show all your cards to the opposition. When Jack Woltz shows Tom Hagen his prize horse, it displays a vulnerability that Hagen, of course, is able to exploit in one of the most horrifying scenes in the movie. And when Don Corleone criticizes Sonny after a business meeting, he says, "Never tell anyone outside the family what you are thinking."

MICHAEL: I think those sequences also show us two other important points. First, with Woltz, Tom Hagen demonstrates great business acumen. Although the first meeting is terrible, he ends it by complimenting Woltz's films. He doesn't slam the door no matter how much Woltz insults him. The famous line hasn't been uttered yet, but Hagen lives it in his behavior: This is business, not personal. Woltz, in contrast, makes it all personal. He tells about the actress Johnny stole away. "She made me look ridiculous and a man in my position can't afford to look ridiculous." Hagen never loses his cool or focus and finds Woltz's weakness, the horse.

The Sollozzo meeting shows Sonny contradicting his father, creating the appearance of weakness in the family's unity, which ultimately sets the tragedy of the movie in motion. Sonny unwittingly makes his father appear to be the stumbling block to a major drug deal, and therefore makes him a target for elimination. After the hit, Sollozzo tells Hagen, "Sonny was hot for my deal." Your point about not showing cards is dead on, but it's also important to avoid mixed messages to a business partner or, heaven forbid, a murderous rival. Only bad things happen then.

KEVIN: It isn't only Sonny who makes mistakes, though. The Sollozzo scene also makes us question if Don Corleone made a mistake sending Luca Brasi to try and gather intelligence about the other Mafia family. Luca Brasi simply wasn't credible as a discontented soldier. Isn't that a kind of management error? Vito shouldn't make that kind of mistake.

MICHAEL: I agree, but two other points come through. First, look at how Vito talks to Brasi when it's all about business. It's curt and direct, minus all the trappings of the wedding. That's great situational leadership.

But the Sollozzo meeting shows a major flaw. Vito knows he has a succession problem, which is so painfully common in family businesses.

Sonny clearly can't control his emotions, Fredo isn't up to the job in any way and Vito wants Michael, temperamentally the ideal successor, nowhere near the business. Tom Hagen, while he has been a kind of foster son to Vito, simply has the wrong last name and heritage. Daughter Connie (who in the sequels will show her power) is the wrong sex. Think of how many businesses have gone off the rails when something happens to the powerhouse founder. Companies, and especially small family companies, need a well-defined succession plan.

KEVIN: True. Sort of like Apple Computer or Disney. It can take years to regain momentum after things go bad.

There is a sense—after Michael has committed murder and escaped to Sicily, and before Vito retakes control—that the family business is in chaos. It is clearly because there is no strong, reasoned, and contextual leadership. At this point in the movie the Corleones are practicing reactive management, which is no way to run any sort of business organization.

MICHAEL: That, of course, brings us a scene everyone loves. After the traitor Paulie is killed in a car, hit man Peter Clemenza delivers the classic line. "Leave the gun, take the cannolis." Clemenza's wife asked for a cannoli and he never lost focus.

KEVIN: What a great expression of how to have the right priorities in business. And, by the way, Clemenza delivers a second lesson through food. The scene where Clemenza explains to Michael how to make sauce isn't really about sauce, is it? It's more about assembling all the right ingredients for any enterprise. Here he is, one of the top leaders of the family laying out key details like that. As he explains, there are times anyone might have to feed a large group.

Clemenza's a leader who understands how to work the details.

But from there, we have to go to the hospital scene, where Michael alertly saves his father's life. First, by recognizing the guards are gone. Then, by moving his father and completing the moment by posing with Enzo outside the hospital to create the appearance of muscle. I love the moment when Michael realizes his hands aren't shaking, when he realizes that the mobster life is part of who he is. I wonder how many executives have that same kind of moment when they realize, "I can do this."

MICHAEL: Great point, because a leader has to want leadership. Think of how Ted Kennedy's presidential bid unraveled in 1980 because he could not assertively answer the question of why he wanted the job.

What got me about this scene was watching Michael cope with crisis. Instead of panicking, he builds a creative solution and wins without guns or backup. Faced with a huge problem, he focuses on the solution.

In contrast, Sonny shows his lack of management skill immediately after that scene by escalating the war with the other families. It's clear that all his top advisors—Clemenza, Tessio and Hagen—know he has overreacted, but they can't help him. Hagen tries to offer dissent and Sonny explodes. Too many managers do the same, forgetting that they need to hear opposing views.

KEVIN: The classic line, "This is business, not personal," is uttered by Tom Hagen after Don Corleone is shot, but most people forget Sonny's immediate response: "Business will have to suffer."

This is a more complicated question than people might think. Sure, it is important to keep personal considerations out of business decisions for the most part, but not always. There are times when you have to let personal values affect the business behavior, though clearly, Sonny makes a serious management mistake in letting his emotions run away with him.

MICHAEL: That's a critical point. Leaders sometimes have to make tough decisions and Sonny made one. Of course, there's rarely anything to admire in his management style.

KEVIN: I'd argue that there's at least some indication that Sonny does have his managerial moments. After the family has agreed to let Michael kill Sollozzo and Captain McCluskey, pretty much everyone puts out feelers to find out where the meeting will take place. That's the only way a gun can be planted. In the end it is the boss, Sonny, who has the right connections to get the location. And he does so by taking the unorthodox approach, finding out where the corrupt police captain is going to be, rather than what the mobster's plans are. There's a good lesson that sometimes the top dog has to get involved, use contacts, and deliver.

MICHAEL: That scene also shows us why Michael is such a capable leader. While planning the hit, most everyone considers McCluskey, a police captain, an unassailable foe. Michael argues against that, saying the family has to spread the story of the cop's link to organized crime and narcotics.

KEVIN: True. There's a not-so-old business saying, "There's no such thing as an unassailable advantage." And Michael is smart enough to realize this.

MICHAEL: I love the way Clemenza systematically walks Michael through the killing. It reminds us of the importance of preparation. And, of course, there is Sonny's line about "somebody very good better plant that gun. I don't want my brother coming out of there with just his d**k in his hands." Details always matter.

Many years ago my wife worked in the financial department at General Foods (now part of Kraft). Each year the finance staff had to prepare a special summary for the CEO to ensure he wouldn't get stumped by any question, no matter how detailed, when meeting with shareholders. In short, he couldn't walk up to that podium with anything less than a loaded gun of information in his hands.

KEVIN: After the shooting, Michael hides out in Sicily. The Sicilian sequences are a strong reminder of the importance of getting away from the office. A respite allows you to think about the business from a distance with objectivity. It isn't necessary to be in hiding for more than a year, but the occasional sabbatical certainly makes sense. Of course, the final scenes of the Sicilian sequences suggest that while you can get away from the office, sometimes business follows you home.

Michael's courtship and wedding to Apollonia in Sicily also provide a good example of what sometimes is called "servant leadership," in which Michael respects the institution and traditions more than he tries to assert his power and authority.

MICHAEL: I think Michael learns a painful and common business lesson in Sicily: know the local customs. When he first inquires about Apollonia, he nearly gets into a fight with her father. Too many businesses do this when moving to different cultures. There are classic examples like the Chevrolet Nova that was marketed in Spanish speaking countries without anyone realizing that "no va" means "doesn't go" in Spanish. Michael learns the lesson just in time.

Sadly, he lets his guard down briefly about the ongoing war in America and tragedy ensues in Sicily, just as it has in America.

KEVIN: And when Sonny gets killed at the tollbooth, it is yet another example of what happens when you let your emotions run away with you. You lose perspective, you don't dot the i's and cross the t's and you end up with about a thousand bullets riddling your body. Sometimes really, sometimes metaphorically.

Sonny's killing leads to Vito retaking control; first to bury his son and second to end the war. My first reaction to the scene in which the dons of the five families meet is that it is a terrific example of strong leadership by Don Corleone. While he is there to make peace, he's also able to gauge the situation and identify his real enemies. He presents himself as a reasonable man with a specific goal: "When did I ever refuse an accommodation," and "This war stops now." But he also lets the group know categorically that there are lines that must not be crossed. His tone and words turn sharp as he informs them that this new peace is dependent on Michael's ability to return unharmed from Sicily. If something happens to Michael, he says, "I will not forgive."

MICHAEL: Vito's reemergence is a powerful moment. I find it interesting that he also understood what it took to close the deal on a peace treaty. Up until Sonny's death, the war was one-sided in one important way: Tattaglia's son had been killed, but no Corleone had died. As Vito makes clear in the peace conference, his suffering is now equal to his rival's. A painful peace was possible, although Vito makes it clear that a second son will not suffer.

KEVIN: There's something else interesting about the meeting and it has nothing to do with Corleone. I'm struck by the moment when the one gangster says that he's always objected to getting into the drug rackets, but understands that the Mafia must modernize to survive, provided there are limits. "I don't want it near schools, and I don't want it sold to children." As reprehensible as the general business plan is, it occurs to me as a case of a businessman deciding that there is such a thing as the intelligent loss of business, that sometimes you have to let personal values get in the way of pragmatic business decisions. Of course, we know that eventually drugs do find their way onto school playgrounds, so sometimes the best laid plans...

MICHAEL: Ethics matter, as we've seen repeatedly. The gangster's concerns are well articulated, but it's a reminder that an ethically challenged decision won't work well in the long run. The drug culture never stayed within the bounds the families outline. Good intentions can be difficult to follow.

KEVIN: Certainly Michael shows that he has good intentions when he says to Kay, "In five years the Corleone family is going to be completely legitimate." How often does he say something like that during the three *Godfather* films, but never quite makes it to the finish line? "Just when I thought I was out...they pull me back in," he says in *The Godfather, Part III.*

Michael turns out to be a very different kind of manager and leader than his father. Witness the scene in which he cuts loose Tom Hagen as *consigliore.* There is no sentimentality in his words or actions, even as Vito tries to soften the blow. I suppose there is a good business debate to be had here—who is the better don: Vito or Michael? I vote for Vito, because the business does not seem to corrode his soul the way it does Michael's.

MICHAEL: That is a core question to all three of these movies and the answer is definitely Vito. Remember, this is a family of cold-blooded killers. But Vito's roots are different. He seems to have a higher purpose, caring for his community of fellow immigrants who struggled through the transition to America. Michael shows us no purpose.

KEVIN: This really is only hinted at in *The Godfather,* and we learn more about it in *Part II*. I'm reminded that when Coppola once was asked why he made a sequel, he said it was in part for the money, but also because it allowed him to address the amorality that was so much a part of the original picture.

MICHAEL: As the film unfolds, we do get the sense that however corrupt his ethics may be, Michael seems to have an intuitive sense of how to lead and manage the family business. Remember in the beginning of the film, Vito deals with four wedding guests in very different ways? The same thing happens when Michael goes to Las Vegas.

When he arrives in Las Vegas, he instantly ends Fredo's party, blaming fatigue to avoid further embarrassment for his brother. He talks respectfully to Johnny about the entertainment deal. And then he switches tone and gives Moe Greene the tough talk on a possible buyout and a review of problems.

KEVIN: That scene in Vegas also is a great example of two underlings, Fredo and Moe Greene, forgetting where the real power is and forgetting who the boss is. They have become so isolated, so enmeshed in their own business dealings that they have lost perspective. That's a dangerous occurrence in any business, but arguably worse in a business where errors in judgment are rewarded with a bullet.

Of course, that brings us to the final scenes, the Corleones' revenge on all their past enemies—interspersed with the scenes of Michael at the baptism of Connie's and Carlo's child.

There is an interesting dynamic after the baptism where Michael sits down with Carlo, who we know has been complicit in the murder of Sonny. He wants to hear Carlo admit his role, but to do so, Michael doesn't sit across from him, or stand over him. Rather, he takes a chair and places it next to Carlo. He creates a sense of connection, even intimacy, in order to learn what he needs to know. Once Carlo admits he helped orchestrate Sonny's murder the civility disappears and Carlo soon follows.

MICHAEL: That entire sequence shows us how much Michael learned. He masters the patience, the planning and even the tone that his father employed so well. But what bothers me is the core of what he learned. Vito didn't want his son in the business, yet he left him in charge. Michael knew better, but employed his father's most ruthless means to make his mark.

There's a great parallel to the many companies we've seen challenged by ethics through the years. How is it possible that no one thinks to stop the process? Instead, the practitioners simply get better at skirting the law.

The last lesson in the movie hits that point, when Michael's wife Kay confronts him. Kay knows the truth, yet chooses to avoid it. She buys the lie that is so transparent, especially when the men come in and kiss Michael's hand, clearly signifying their respect for his power. She knows he was responsible and does nothing. It reminds me of the staffs and boards of directors of companies like Enron, AIG, and many others. How often did they know something wasn't right and refused to ask the hard questions or even question whether they were getting the truth?

Maybe that's ultimately the difference between a movie that is simply entertainment and one that is great—the latter uses the language and pictures of art to comment on transcendent themes and ideas.

KEVIN: The fact that *The Godfather* is such a great movie is a testament to how important luck is in any enterprise. After all, if things had turned out differently, *The Godfather* might have starred Laurence Olivier or Ernest Borgnine as Don Corleone, Burt Reynolds as Sonny, and James Caan as Michael. Francis Ford Coppola wasn't even the first choice to be director. Originally the studio wanted Sergio Leone or Peter Bogdanovich to direct.

There's something to be said for both luck and alchemy—part of any good business enterprise is assembling all the right parts and then making sure they all work together.

The Godfather works.

Final Shot

In every movie, there's a closing scene. The goal of that moment is to wrap things up, to leave the audience with a sense of closure.

So here's our final shot.

Different people respond to different narratives. Business lessons abound in movies that aren't movies about business. We want you to find the metaphors in the movies that will resonate with you and the people with whom you need to communicate.

Looking for a way to illustrate the concept of bringing a new perspective to your business? Try the movie *Dave*. It's the comedy in which Kevin Kline plays the body double for a U.S. president, and then finds himself occupying the Oval Office when the nation's chief executive has a stroke. During his time in the White House, Dave and his accountant, hilariously played by Charles Grodin, bring fresh eyes to the nation's problems and policies and actually achieve something. That's a great business lesson.

Dave creates a president—at least, when he's being impersonated—that real Americans can identify with. That's another business lesson: the importance of putting a face on the institution.

If you need a movie to demonstrate the problem of what can happen when you don't pay attention to the signs around you, there's *The Perfect Storm*. The movie chronicles the ill fortune of Captain Billy Tyne (played by George Clooney) of the Andrea Gail, a hard-luck fishing boat out of Gloucester, Massachusetts. Tyne is aware of the bad weather, and is urged not to sail into the approaching storm, but he has a kind of myopia familiar to many business people—he is so focused on catching fish to make up for consistently poor performances that he ignores all the warning signs and disaster occurs.

Contrasting the careers of Clint Eastwood and Burt Reynolds, two actors who are roughly the same age and who both came up in the same studio system of the 1950s, provides an excellent example of how to create a strong brand and viable business model—and how not to. Three guesses which one got it right. Need a hint? Eastwood made *Million Dollar Baby*. Reynolds did guest shots on *My Name Is Earl*.

You can look at Hollywood's own business practices for a cautionary note. One of the movie industry's worst habits is to return to the same story time after time after time. There seems to be a shortage of good ideas in Hollywood, and the movie industry can be notably risk-averse. Even a bad idea poorly executed doesn't seem so bad if it is based on an idea that previously made some money. But it rarely works, as movies like *Fatal Attraction II*, *Jaws 2*, *Jaws 3-D*, and *The Sting II* make clear. (You'd think *The Sting II*, which had Jackie Gleason and Mac Davis playing the roles originally played by Paul Newman and Robert Redford, would have been enough to put Hollywood off sequels forever. But most studio execs probably don't even remember that such a film was made.)

We could go on and on.

So we hope you can take some of the lessons we've illustrated in this book to your company when the situation arises that you need to say, "That is just like the story in…" Now these tales are yours, too.

And we'll see you at the multiplex.

APPENDIX A: ALPHABETICAL LISTING OF MOVIES

All About Eve (1950)
Directed by Joseph L. Mankiewicz
Written by Joseph L. Mankiewicz
Starring Bette Davis, Anne Baxter,
George Sanders
Not Rated

All the President's Men (1976)
Directed by Alan J. Pakula
Written by William Goldman,
based on the book by Carl
Bernstein and Bob Woodward
Starring Dustin Hoffman, Robert
Redford, Jason Robards
Rated PG

Amadeus (1984)
Directed by Milos Forman
Written by Peter Shaffer
Starring F. Murray Abraham, Tom
Hulce, Elizabeth Berridge
Rated PG

American Gangster (2007)
Directed by Ridley Scott
Written by Steven Zaillian, based
on an article by Mark Jacobson
Starring Denzel Washington,
Russell Crowe, Chiwetel Ejiofor
Rated R

Appaloosa (2008)
Directed by Ed Harris
Written by Robert Knott and Ed
Harris, based on the novel by
Robert B. Parker
Starring Ed Harris, Viggo
Mortensen, Renee Zellweger
Rated R

Babe (1995)
Directed by Chris Noonan
Written by George Miller and
Chris Noonan, based on the novel
by Dick King-Smith
Starring James Cromwell, Magda
Szubanski, voice of Christine
Cavanaugh
Rated G

Big (1988)
Directed by Penny Marshall
Written by Gary Ross and Anne
Spielberg
Starring Tom Hanks, Elizabeth
Perkins, Robert Loggia
Rated PG

Big Night (1996)
Directed by Campbell Scott and
Stanley Tucci
Written by Joseph Tropiano and
Stanley Tucci
Starring Marc Anthony, Tony
Shalhoub, Stanley Tucci
Rated R

Bottle Shock (2008)
Directed by Randall Miller
Written by Jody Savin, Randall
Miller, Ross Schwartz
Starring Chris Pine, Alan Rickman,
Bill Pullman
Rated PG-13

The Bridge on the River Kwai
(1957)
Directed by David Lean
Written by Michael Wilson and
Carl Foreman, based on the novel
by Pierre Boulle
Starring William Holden, Alec
Guinness, Jack Hawkins
Not Rated

Broadcast News (1987)
Directed by James L. Brooks
Written by James L. Brooks
Starring William Hurt, Albert
Brooks, Holly Hunter
Rated R

Bull Durham (1988)
Directed by Ron Shelton
Written by Ron Shelton
Starring Kevin Costner, Susan
Sarandon, Tim Robbins
Rated R

*Butch Cassidy and the Sundance
Kid* (1969)
Directed by George Roy Hill
Written by William Goldman
Starring Paul Newman, Robert
Redford, Katharine Ross
Rated PG

The Caine Mutiny (1954)
Directed by Edward Dmytryk
Written by Stanley Roberts, based
on the novel by Herman Wouk
Starring Humphrey Bogart, Jose
Ferrer, Van Johnson
Not Rated

Casablanca (1942)
Directed by Michael Curtiz
Written by Julius J. Epstein, Philip
G. Epstein, Howard Koch, based
on the play by Murray Burnett and
Joan Alison
Starring Humphrey Bogart, Ingrid
Bergman, Paul Henreid
Not Rated

Casino Royale (2006)
Directed by Martin Campbell
Written by Neal Purvis, Robert
Wade, Paul Haggis, based on the
novel by Ian Fleming
Starring Daniel Craig, Eva Green,
Mads Mikkelsen
Rated PG-13

Charlie Wilson's War (2007)
Directed by Mike Nichols
Written by Aaron Sorkin, based on
the book by George Crile
Starring Tom Hanks, Julia Roberts,
Philip Seymour Hoffman
Rated R

Citizen Kane (1941)
Directed by Orson Welles
Written by Herman J. Mankiewicz
and Orson Welles
Starring Orson Welles, Joseph
Cotton, Dorothy Comingore
Rated PG

Cool Runnings (1993)
Directed by Jon Turteltaub
Written by Lynn Siefert, Tommy
Swerdlow, Michael Goldberg
Starring John Candy, Leon
Robinson, Doug E. Doug
Rated PG

Defending Your Life (1991)
Directed by Albert Brooks
Written by Albert Brooks
Starring Albert Brooks, Meryl
Streep, Rip Torn
Rated PG

50 First Dates (2004)
Directed by Peter Segal
Written by George Wing
Starring Adam Sandler, Drew
Barrymore, Rob Schneider
Rated PG-13

Gandhi (1982)
Directed by Richard Attenborough
Written by John Briley
Starring Ben Kingsley, Candice
Bergen, Edward Fox
Rated PG

The Godfather (1972)
Directed by Francis Ford Coppola
Written by Mario Puzo and Francis
Ford Coppola, based on the novel
by Mario Puzo
Starring Marlon Brando, Al Pacino,
James Caan
Rated R

Good Night, and Good Luck
(2005)
Directed by George Clooney
Written by George Clooney and
Grant Heslov
Starring David Strathairn, George
Clooney, Robert Downey, Jr.
Rated PG

The Guns of Navarone (1961)
Directed by J. Lee Thompson
Written by Carl Foreman, based on
the novel by Alistair MacLean
Starring Gregory Peck, David
Niven, Anthony Quinn
Not Rated

Guys and Dolls (1955)
Directed by Joseph L. Mankiewicz
Written by Joseph L. Mankiewicz,
based on the play by Jo Swerling
and Abe Burrows
Starring Marlon Brando, Jean
Simmons, Frank Sinatra
Not Rated

He's Just Not That Into You (2009)
Directed by Ken Kwapis
Written by Abby Kohn and Marc
Silverstein, based on the book by
Greg Behrendt and Liz Tuccillo
Starring Jennifer Aniston, Ben
Affleck, Bradley Cooper
Rated PG-13

High Noon (1952)
Directed by Fred Zinnemann
Written by Carl Foreman, based
on the magazine story by John W.
Cunningham
Starring Gary Cooper, Grace Kelly,
Lloyd Bridges
Not Rated

Hoosiers (1986)
Directed by David Anspaugh
Written by Angelo Pizzo
Starring Gene Hackman, Barbara
Hershey, Dennis Hopper
Rated PG

In the Heat of the Night (1967)
Directed by Norman Jewison
Written by Stirling Silliphant,
based on the novel by John Ball
Starring Sidney Poitier, Rod Steiger,
Warren Oates
Not Rated

Jaws (1975)
Directed by Steven Spielberg
Written by Peter Benchley and
Carl Gottlieb, based on the novel
by Peter Benchley
Starring Roy Scheider, Robert
Shaw, Richard Dreyfuss
Rated PG

Julie & Julia (2009)
Directed by Nora Ephron
Written by Nora Ephron, based
on a book by Julie Powell and
a book by Julia Child and Alex
Prud'homme
Starring Meryl Streep, Amy Adams,
Stanley Tucci
Rated PG-13

Jurassic Park (1993)
Directed by Steven Spielberg
Written by Michael Crichton and
David Koepp, based on the novel
by Michael Crichton
Starring Sam Neill, Laura Dern, Jeff
Goldblum
Rated PG-13

A League of Their Own (1992)
Directed by Penny Marshall
Written by Lowell Ganz and
Babaloo Mandel
Starring Tom Hanks, Geena Davis,
Madonna
Rated PG

The Man Who Would Be King
(1975)
Directed by John Huston
Written by John Huston and
Gladys Hill, based on the short
story by Rudyard Kipling
Starring Sean Connery, Michael
Caine, Christopher Plummer
Rated PG

Misery (1990)
Directed by Rob Reiner
Written by William Goldman,
based on the novel by Stephen
King
Starring James Caan, Kathy Bates,
Richard Farnsworth
Rated R

Mister Roberts (1955)
Directed by John Ford and Mervyn
LeRoy
Written by Frank S. Nugent and
Joshua Logan, based on the novel
by Thomas Heggen and play by
Thomas Heggen and Joshua Logan
Starring Henry Fonda, James
Cagney, William Powell
Not Rated

Network (1976)
Directed by Sidney Lumet
Written by Paddy Chayefsky
Starring Faye Dunaway, William
Holden, Peter Finch
Rated R

*Pirates of the Caribbean: The
Curse of the Black Pearl* (2003)
Directed by Gore Verbinski
Written by Ted Elliot and Terry
Rossio
Starring Johnny Depp, Geoffrey
Rush, Orlando Bloom
Rated PG-13

The Producers (1968)
Directed by Mel Brooks
Written by Mel Brooks
Starring Zero Mostel, Gene Wilder,
Kenneth Mars
Rated PG

Pumping Iron (1977)
Directed by George Butler and
Robert Fiore
Written by Charles Gaines and
George Butler
Starring Arnold Schwarzenegger,
Lou Ferrigno, Mike Katz
Rated PG

Quantum of Solace (2008)
Directed by Marc Forster
Written by Paul Haggis, Neal
Purvis, Robert Wade
Starring Daniel Craig, Olga
Kurylenko, Mathieu Amalric
Rated PG-13

Renaissance Man (1994)
Directed by Penny Marshall
Written by Jim Burnstein
Starring Danny DeVito, Gregory
Hines, James Remar
Rated PG-13

The Right Stuff (1983)
Directed by Philip Kaufman
Written by Philip Kaufman, based
on the book by Tom Wolfe
Starring Sam Shepard, Scott Glenn,
Ed Harris
Rated PG

Robin and Marian (1976)
Directed by Richard Lester
Written by James Goldman
Starring Sean Connery, Audrey
Hepburn, Robert Shaw
Rated PG

Rocky (1976)
Directed by John G. Avildsen
Written by Sylvester Stallone
Starring Sylvester Stallone, Talia
Shire, Burt Young
Rated PG

Schindler's List (1993)
Directed by Steven Spielberg
Written by Steven Zaillian, based
on the book by Thomas Keneally
Starring Liam Neeson, Ben
Kingsley, Ralph Fiennes
Rated R

Selena (1997)
Directed by Gregory Nava
Written by Gregory Nava
Starring Jennifer Lopez, Jackie
Guerra, Edward James Olmos
Rated PG

Sex and the City (2008)
Directed by Michael Patrick King
Written by Michael Patrick King,
based on the book by Candace
Bushnell
Starring Sarah Jessica Parker, Kim
Cattrall, Kristin Davis, Cynthia
Nixon
Rated R

The Shawshank Redemption
(1994)
Directed by Frank Darabont
Written by Frank Darabont, based
on the short story by Stephen King
Starring Tim Robbins, Morgan
Freeman, Bob Gunton
Rated R

Star Trek V: The Final Frontier
(1989)
Directed by William Shatner
Written by David Loughery, based
on the television series by Gene
Roddenberry
Starring William Shatner, Leonard
Nimoy, DeForest Kelley
Rated PG

*Star Trek VI: The Undiscovered
Country* (1991)
Directed by Nicholas Meyer
Written by Nicholas Meyer and
Denny Martin Flinn, based on
the television series by Gene
Roddenberry
Starring William Shatner, Leonard
Nimoy, DeForest Kelley
Rated PG

Stranger than Fiction (2006)
Directed by Marc Forster
Written by Zach Helm
Starring Will Ferrell, Emma
Thompson, Dustin Hoffman
Rated PG-13

*Talladega Nights: The Ballad of
Ricky Bobby* (2006)
Directed by Adam McKay
Written by Adam McKay and Will
Ferrell
Starring Will Ferrell, John C. Reilly,
Gary Cole
PG-13

That Thing You Do! (1996)
Directed by Tom Hanks
Written by Tom Hanks
Starring Tom Everett Scott, Liv
Tyler, Johnathon Schaech
Rated PG

Tin Cup (1996)
Directed by Ron Shelton
Written by John Norville and Ron
Shelton
Starring Kevin Costner, Rene
Russo, Don Johnson
Rated R

Tootsie (1982)
Directed by Sydney Pollack
Written by Murray Schisgal and
Larry Gelbart
Starring Dustin Hoffman, Jessica
Lange, Teri Garr
Rated PG

Tucker: The Man and His Dream
(1988)
Directed by Francis Ford Coppola
Written by Arnold Schulman and
David Seidler
Starring Jeff Bridges, Joan Allen,
Martin Landau
Rated PG

The Untouchables (1987)
Directed by Brian De Palma
Written by David Mamet
Starring Kevin Costner, Sean
Connery, Robert DeNiro
Rated R

The Wedding Singer (1998)
Directed by Frank Coraci
Written by Tim Herlihy
Starring Adam Sandler, Drew
Barrymore, Christine Taylor
Rated PG-13

When Harry Met Sally (1989)
Directed by Rob Reiner
Written by Nora Ephron
Starring Billy Crystal, Meg Ryan,
Carrie Fisher
Rated R

The Wind and the Lion (1975)
Written by John Milius
Directed by John Milius
Starring Sean Connery, Candice
Bergen, Brian Keith
Rated PG

Working Girl (1988)
Directed by Mike Nichols
Written by Kevin Wade
Starring Harrison Ford, Sigourney
Weaver, Melanie Griffith
Rated R

You've Got Mail (1998)
Directed by Nora Ephron
Written by Nora Ephron and Delia
Ephron, based on a play by Miklos
Laszlo
Starring Tom Hanks, Meg Ryan,
Greg Kinnear
Rated PG

Young Frankenstein (1974)
Directed by Mel Brooks
Written by Gene Wilder and Mel
Brooks
Starring Gene Wilder, Peter Boyle,
Marty Feldman
Rated PG

APPENDIX B: BUSINESS RATINGS

If you're looking for a movie to illustrate a point you want to make in
your company, check this list.

BRANDING
American Gangster
Big Night
Bottle Shock
Casino Royale
Julie & Julia
The Man Who Would Be King
Pirates of the Caribbean: The
Curse of the Black Pearl
Pumping Iron
Quantum of Solace
Robin and Marian
Sex and the City
That Thing That You Do!
Tootsie
Tucker: The Man and His Dream
The Untouchables
The Wind and the Lion
You've Got Mail

RULE BREAKERS
All About Eve
All the President's Men
Amadeus
Babe
Butch Cassidy and the Sundance Kid
The Caine Mutiny
Casino Royale
Charlie Wilson's War
Citizen Kane
Cool Runnings
Defending Your Life
50 First Dates
Gandhi
Guys and Dolls
He's Just Not That Into You

The Man Who Would Be King
Mister Roberts
Misery
Network
Pirates of the Caribbean: The
Curse of the Black Pearl
The Producers
Quantum of Solace
The Right Stuff
Robin and Marian
Rocky
Schindler's List
Star Trek V: The Final Frontier
Stranger than Fiction
Talladega Nights: The Legend of
Ricky Bobby
Tin Cup
Tucker: The Man and His Dream
The Untouchables
The Wedding Singer
The Wind and the Lion
Working Girl
Young Frankenstein

CUSTOMER FOCUS
Big
Big Night
Bottle Shock
50 First Dates
Julie & Julia
Selena
That Thing You Do!
Tucker: The Man and His Dream
The Wedding Singer
When Harry Met Sally
You've Got Mail

ETHICS
All About Eve
All the President's Men
Appaloosa
The Bridge on the River Kwai
Broadcast News
Casablanca
Gandhi
The Godfather
Good Night, and Good Luck
High Noon
Hoosiers
In the Heat of the Night
Jurassic Park
Misery
Schindler's List
Sex and the City
Star Trek V: The Final Frontier
Star Trek VI: The Undiscovered Country
Stranger than Fiction
Working Girl

LEADERSHIP
A League of Their Own
All the President's Men
Big Night
The Bridge on the River Kwai
Bull Durham
Butch Cassidy and the Sundance Kid
The Caine Mutiny
Charlie Wilson's War
Citizen Kane
Cool Runnings
Defending Your Life
Gandhi
The Godfather

The Guns of Navarone
Hoosiers
In the Heat of the Night
Jaws
Jurassic Park
The Man Who Would Be King
Mister Roberts
Network
Pirates of the Caribbean: The Curse of the Black Pearl
The Producers
Renaissance Man
The Right Stuff
Robin and Marian
Rocky
Schindler's List
Star Trek VI: The Undiscovered Country
Tucker: The Man and His Dream
The Untouchables
The Wind and the Lion

PLANNING
Butch Cassidy and the Sundance Kid
Casablanca
The Godfather
The Guns of Navarone
Jaws
The Producers
Rocky
The Shawshank Redemption
Star Trek VI: The Undiscovered Country
That Thing You Do!
Working Girl
Young Frankenstein

Acknowledgments

So, who gets mentioned in the acknowledgments?

Best I can figure, it probably should be all the people who didn't make the dedication. And when you've waited until your mid-fifties to publish your first book, you better cram as many people in as possible on the off chance that there is no second book…

I haven't seen him or talked to him in more than 30 years, but Mike Callahan, my old film professor at Loyola Marymount University, was the first person to suggest to me that I could write *about* movies as well as actually write movies. Since none of my screenplays have ever been produced, and I've slipped movie references into much of my journalism for the past three decades, I'm glad he did.

Vic Magnotta didn't live long enough to see all this happen, but hardly a week goes by when I don't think of him and hear him say, "Keep smiling."

The writers who continue to inspire me with their prose: Robert B. Parker, Michael Connelly, Pete Hamill. Their words are like music that I can't get out of my head.

I've learned a lot about business and much more from a number of people over the years that I have been privileged to call my friends: Tony Kiser, Jim Donald, Feargal Quinn, Richard and Linda Coulter.

All the great friends who have made the ride first class: Rich and Barbara Davis, Mike and Lynn Wellman, Stu and Kate Upson, Fiach and Anne O'Broin, and Tony Stanton.

There is, of course, my family of birth…my Dad, who has never quite understood what I do for a living, my Mom, who left us way too early, and my six brothers and sisters, who keep me grounded. And,

there is my family of choice, Jim and Joan Roxbury, who laugh at the jokes, share the meals and the drinks, and are always there...even when they're not.

And thanks, of course, to Michael...who made me finally get it done.

Kevin Coupe

It's a lucky person who has so many people to thank he doesn't know where to stop. Luckily, I know where to start. Thanks to Mom and Dad for the love of movies, stories and education. To Robin and Marcy for being the best friends and sisters a guy could have.

Thanks to Glenn Snyder and Steve Weinstein for guidance. To Elaine Sherman, Joy Nicholas, Pat Shinko, Ernie Monschein, Anne-Marie Roerink and Sherrie Rosenblatt for making the office a place to enjoy.

I've been fortunate to work with and learn from incredible business leaders including Danny Wegman, Stew Leonard (Senior and Junior), Tres Lund, Craig Schnuck, Norman Mayne, Ed Crenshaw, Leonard Harris, Joe Colalillo, Bill McEwan, Tim Smucker, Bob Bartels, Tim Hammonds, Don Knauss, Sandy Douglas, Bill Grize, and the brilliant Noddle brothers, Allan and Jeff. To friends like Joe Burke, Denny Bel Castro, Ryan Wall, Rose Mitchell, Mark Thorngren, Tom Joyce, Sandy Brawley, Phil Lempert, and Frank Gambino. I'm happy to say there are too many more who deserve to be listed, but space doesn't permit it, so forgive me if I missed you.

To Susan, Adam and Jack for devotion to the New York Mets. To Kay Coon, her kids, grandkids, and great-grandkids who will all be receiving copies of this book as gifts.

To Neil and Janis for making a book idea become reality; and to Kevin for making me laugh at almost every step of the process.

And, of course, thanks to you for reading.

Michael Sansolo

About the Authors

KEVIN COUPE has been a working writer all his professional life. For the past decade, he's had his own website/blog—*www.MorningNewsBeat.com*—providing what he calls "business news in context, and analysis with attitude."

In addition to speaking at hundreds of conferences in the U.S. and abroad and reporting from 45 states and six continents, Kevin has been a newspaper reporter, video producer, actor, bodyguard, clothing salesman, supervised a winery tasting room, ran two marathons (slowly), drove a race car (badly), took boxing lessons (painfully), and acted in a major (and obscure) motion picture.

Kevin is married with three children and lives in Connecticut. He can be reached at kc@kevincoupe.com.

MICHAEL SANSOLO has traveled around the world one supermarket at a time, yet stopped to climb the Sydney Harbour Bridge, the Great Wall of China, and Pikes Peak. A native New Yorker, Michael started as a newspaper reporter and somehow became a public speaker on cooking, shopping, and eating trends. Favorite books: this one, and *The Great Gatsby;* favorite food: Sal's Pizza; favorite team: The Mets; favorite reader: you; favorite movies: just read the book!

Michael, his family, and his very annoying beagle live in the suburbs of Washington, D.C. His website is *www.MichaelSansolo.com* and you can email him at michael@michaelsansolo.com. Donate blood—it helps!